TAKING THE
KALACHAKRA INITIATION

TAKING THE KALACHAKRA INITIATION

by
Alexander Berzin

Foreword by
His Holiness the Dalai Lama

Snow Lion Publications
Ithaca, New York

Snow Lion Publications
P.O. Box 6483
Ithaca, New York 14851 USA
607-273-8519

First edition USA 1997

Printed in Canada on acid-free, recycled paper.

ISBN 1-55939-084-0

Library of Congress Cataloging-in-Publication Data
Berzin, Alexander.
    Taking the Kalachakra initiation / by Alexander Berzin ; foreword
by His Holiness the Dalai Lama.
       p.   cm.
    Includes bibliographical references.
    ISBN 1-55939-084-0
    1. Kālacakra (Tantric rite) I. Title
    BQ8921.K34B47   1997
    294.3'438--dc21   97-37384
                                                            CIP

 PRINTED IN CANADA

Table of Contents

THE DALAI LAMA

Foreword

Throughout the world there is a deeply felt need for both external and internal peace. The Kalachakra initiation is a profound ceremony that gathers and unites people from all nations and backgrounds in a peaceful, spiritual activity that affects both those people and the environment in a significant and constructive manner. For this reason, several lamas, including myself, have been happy to confer the initiation when requested.

In preparing this guidebook, Alexander Berzin has done a great service to everyone interested in the Kalachakra initiation. It will help people who receive the initiation from lamas of any of the four lineages of Tibetan Buddhism to prepare for the ceremony and understand the essential points of each step of the procedure. By explaining clearly the Kalachakra path of spiritual development, as well as the vows and commitments involved, the book will help people to make a realistic decision about whether to take the empowerment as a full participant or merely as an observer. Many people who are not yet ready to engage in Kalachakra meditation practice, and many who are not even Buddhists but have sincere wishes for peace, attend the initiation as interested observers. I am especially happy that the book addresses this section of the audience as well, suggesting ways in which they can make the experience more meaningful.

It is my prayer that everyone who plans to attend, or has ever attended a Kalachakra initiation may ultimately reap the full benefit of doing so.

April 8, 1997

Preface

For several decades, masters from all four lineages of Tibetan Buddhism have been conferring the Kalachakra initiation in India, Mongolia, Southeast Asia and the West. Thousands of people from Buddhist and non-Buddhist cultures alike have either received the empowerment as active participants or attended as interested observers. Requests for future Kalachakra initiations from around the world are ever-increasing. The interest is great.

Only a handful of Westerners attended the first Kalachakra empowerment His Holiness the Dalai Lama conferred outside Tibet, and I had the good fortune to be among them. This was in Dharamsala, India, in March 1970. Seeing that many more Westerners would come to future initiations, His Holiness decided to make available some guidelines and background information about Kalachakra for this new audience. Thus several months before the Kalachakra empowerment he next conferred in Bodh Gaya, India, in December 1974, His Holiness commissioned Sharpa Rinpochey and myself to translate a series of articles on Kalachakra written by Geshey Ngawang Dhargyey and Garjang Kamtrul Rinpochey. The Library of Tibetan Works & Archives published them in Dharamsala, and Deer Park reprinted the one by Geshey Dhargyey as part of the manual they prepared for His Holiness's first conferral of the initiation in the West. This was in Madison, Wisconsin, in July 1981. Organizers of later Kalachakra initiations have frequently reprinted this manual both in English and several European languages. His Holiness also commissioned Professor Jeffrey Hopkins to translate and publish the text of the initiation ritual so that participants could follow more easily.

His Holiness's main Kalachakra teacher was Tsenzhab Serkong Rinpochey, his late master debate partner and assistant tutor. Serkong Rinpochey was the son and spiritual heir of Serkong Dorjeychang, an outstanding master of Kalachakra and a member of its lineage. Serkong Rinpochey was also my own root guru, whom I served for many years as interpreter. Seeing that there would be ever-growing interest in the West about Kalachakra, he taught me the subject extensively. This included not only formal teaching on its many commentaries, but informal explanations on Kalachakra equivalents to almost anything I translated for him. He never tired of discussing the topic and did so at home, on the road and even at the dinner table, both in India and everywhere we traveled on his lecture tours of the West. He particularly delighted in the details of the three-dimensional Kalachakra mandala palace and would often use dough to make models of its architectural features. I eventually shared these teachings with Martin Brauen in Switzerland, where they became the basis for his book on the topic, and resulted in the construction of a three-dimensional mandala palace at Zurich's Völkerkunde Museum at the time of His Holiness's conferral of the initiation in Rikon, in July 1985.

Wishing me to have a closer link with the lineage, Serkong Rinpochey kindly arranged for me to receive private teachings on Kalachakra from Yongdzin Ling Rinpochey, the late Senior Tutor of His Holiness and a member of the Kalachakra lineage from whom His Holiness received the empowerment. By the time His Holiness conferred the Kalachakra initiation in Spiti, India, in July 1983, I was sufficiently prepared to serve as His Holiness's translator for it. At the time, I felt as if I were an offering made by Serkong Rinpochey to His Holiness for this purpose, and I was filled with an overwhelming feeling of responsibility, awe, respect, gratitude and inspiration.

The last conversation I had with Serkong Rinpochey shortly after that initiation concerned some difficult points about the Kalachakra initiation. He did not quote any commentaries, but worked out the answers to my questions purely with reason. I have taken this as a precious guideline in my own subsequent efforts to teach.

After the deaths of Serkong and Ling Rinpocheys in 1983, His Holiness generously consented to guide my continuing studies and practice of Kalachakra. With Serkong Rinpochey I had begun a program of reading the major commentaries from masters of the four Tibetan lineages, and His Holiness met with me privately to answer questions after I completed each text. Shortly before he passed away, Serkong

Rinpochey had recommended that I study Kalachakra astronomy and astrology with Gen Lodro Gyatso, the late Master Astrologer of the Tibetan Medical and Astrological Institute, and Kalachakra ritual with Lobpön Thubten Choephel, the Kalachakra master of His Holiness's Namgyal Monastery. Following Serkong Rinpochey's death, I followed his advice to round out my Kalachakra education.

In 1985, several Buddhist centers in Europe requested me to give introductory talks on Kalachakra to help people prepare for the initiation which His Holiness would give in July of that year in Rikon, Switzerland. After granting authorization, His Holiness guided me extensively on how to answer the most frequently asked questions. During that initiation, I gave three lectures to help participants and observers through the procedures. Meridian Trust prepared and distributed video tapes of these lectures and the Dharma Friendship Foundation eventually published a lightly edited transcript of them. Subsequent to this initiation, many Buddhist centers in Europe and North America began inviting me to explain basic Kalachakra teachings and meditation practice. Once more, His Holiness was extremely generous with his time and guided me in what and how to teach. Some of the German, French and Dutch lectures were published in those languages by the Aryatara Institut of Munich, Germany, the Vajrayogini Institut of Lavaur, France, and the Maitreya Instituut of Emst, Holland. The main part of the present book is an expansion of the lectures I gave on those tours and the ones I gave at Rikon.

Over the ensuing years, I have had the privilege to serve His Holiness several more times as a translator for the Kalachakra initiation, and as a lecturer during the procedures. During several visits to Mongolia and the former Soviet Union, I spoke with monk and lay scholars about the history of Kalachakra in their countries, and found many rare Kalachakra texts in their libraries. As a result of these visits, the translators for the Kalachakra empowerment His Holiness conferred in Ulaan Baatar, Mongolia, in July 1995, requested me to compile a summary of the ritual to help them prepare. An edited version forms the last chapter of this present work.

In 1996, Sidney Piburn of Snow Lion Publications approached me to expand my previously published work on Kalachakra and compile a more comprehensive book on the topic. His wish was to help those who plan to attend future initiations, and those who had already received the empowerment, to make their experience more meaningful. This book is the result of that request and the long history that preceded it. I wish to thank the Kapor Family Foundation for funding its preparation, and the Nama Rupa Foundation for administering the funds. I also wish to thank my editors at Snow Lion, as well as Rajinder Kumar Dogra and Aldemar Hegewald, for their helpful suggestions. May this book in some way begin to repay the kindness of my teachers and make the world of Kalachakra more accessible for the benefit of all.

Alexander Berzin
Dharamsala, India
February 22, 1997

CHAPTER ONE
Introduction to Tantra

THE NEED FOR A REALISTIC APPROACH

Becoming a Buddha, someone who is totally awake, means to over-come all shortcomings and realize all potentials for the sake of help-ing others. With so much suffering in the world, we urgently need to find the most effective methods to accomplish this goal. The Kalachakra initiation offers an opportunity to meet with such methods. The Ti-betan word for initiation, *wang*, means power, and an initiation is, more accurately, an empowerment. It confers the power and ability to en-gage in certain meditative practices for achieving enlightenment, and thus becoming a Buddha, in order to benefit others as fully as possible.

Kalachakra is a meditational system from the highest level of Bud-dhist tantra, *anuttarayoga*. Some people have odd notions about tantra and imagine, with great anticipation, that an initiation is an entranceway into a magic world of exotic sex and superpowers. When they learn that this is not the case, but rather that tantric practice is complex, advanced and requires serious commitment and the keep-ing of many vows, they become frightened and are put off. Neither of these reactions, of excitement or fear, is appropriate. We need to ap-proach tantra and the Kalachakra initiation in a sensible manner. As my main teacher, Tsenzhab Serkong Rinpochey, once said, "If you prac-tice fantasized methods, you get fantasized results. If you practice re-alistic methods, you get realistic results."

WHAT IS TANTRA?

The word *tantra* means an everlasting stream of continuity. Everlasting streams operate on three levels: as a basis, a pathway and a result. On the basis level, the everlasting stream is our mind — specifically its subtlest level known as primordial clear light — which provides continuity throughout all our lifetimes. Like a pure laser beam of mere clarity and awareness, unadulterated by the gross oscillations of conceptual thought or disturbing emotions, it underlies each moment of experience, whether we are awake or asleep. If mind is like a radio that plays forever, its subtlest level is similar to the machine simply being on. A radio remains on throughout the process of leaving a station, being between bands and tuning into another frequency. Similarly, our subtlest mind never turns off and so is the basis for our experiences of death, *bardo* (the state between rebirths) and the conception of a new life. Neither station, volume, nor even temporary static affects the fact that the radio is on. Likewise, neither rebirth status, intensity of experience, nor even the "fleeting stains" of passing thoughts or moods affect our clear light mind. This subtlest mind proceeds even into Buddhahood and provides the basis for attaining enlightenment.

Furthermore, each stream of continuity, whether prior to enlightenment or afterwards, is individual. All radios are not the same radio, although each receiver works the same. Thus, there is no such thing as a universal clear light mind or basis tantra in which each of our minds participates.

The second level of tantra, the everlasting pathway stream, refers to a specific method for becoming a Buddha, namely meditative practices involving Buddha-figures. This method is sometimes called "deity yoga." The third level, the everlasting resultant stream, is the endless continuity of Buddha-bodies we achieve with enlightenment. To fully help others requires bodies or collections of knowledge, wisdom, experience and forms to suit every being and occasion. In short, tantra involves an everlasting stream of practice with Buddha-figures to purify our everlasting mind-stream of its fleeting stains, in order to achieve, on its basis, the everlasting stream of the bodies of a Buddha. The texts that discuss these topics are also called tantras.

DEITY YOGA

Sometimes people are puzzled by the tantric practice of relying on deities, which some languages translate as "gods." These deities, however, are not omnipotent creators or beings in limited states of rebirth filled with heavenly delights. Rather, they are extraordinary forms, both male and female, in which Buddhas manifest in order to help people with varying inclinations to overcome their shortcomings and realize their potentials. Each of these Buddha-figures represents both the fully enlightened state and one of its specific features, such as compassion or wisdom. Avalokiteshvara, for instance, is a manifestation of compassion, and Manjushri is an embodiment of wisdom. Kalachakra represents the ability to handle all situations at any time. Meditative practice structured around one of these figures and the feature it represents provides a clear focus and framework enabling more rapid progress toward enlightenment than meditation without them.

To alleviate the sufferings of others as quickly as possible requires the most efficient method for gaining the enlightening faculties of a Buddha's body, speech and mind. The basis for achieving them is a strong determination to be free of limitations, non-fickle love and compassion, ethical self-discipline, strict concentration, firm understanding of reality and skill in various means to help others. Once we achieve a working level of these, we need to combine and perfect them so that they bear their results. Tantra provides such a technique, namely deity yoga. Like performing the dress rehearsal for a drama, we imagine we already possess the entire array of these enlightening faculties as a Buddha-figure, all together at the same time. Doing so acts as an effective cause for integrating these qualities and achieving such a form more quickly.

This is an advanced technique. We cannot possibly imagine having all the assets of a Buddha simultaneously unless we have first practiced each individually. We need to learn and rehearse each scene before we can run through an entire play. Therefore, it is both inappropriate and unwise to attempt tantric practice without considerable meditative experience beforehand.

TRAINING THE IMAGINATION

Tantric practice harnesses the imagination — a powerful tool we all possess. Thus, to repeatedly imagine achieving a goal is a compelling method for accomplishing it sooner. Suppose, for example, we are unemployed. If, each day, we imagine finding a job, we succeed more quickly than if we dwell, with depression and self-pity, on being out of work. This is because we maintain a positive attitude about our situation. With a negative attitude, we lack self-confidence even to look for a job. Success or failure in life hinges on our self-image and, in tantra, we work on improving ours by means of Buddha-figures. Imagining we are already a Buddha provides an extremely potent self-image to counteract negative habits and feelings of inadequacy.

The tantric technique does not involve simply the power of positive thinking. When using imagination, it is essential to be practical and maintain a clear distinction between fantasy and reality. Otherwise, serious psychological trouble may arise. Thus every teacher and text emphasizes that an indispensable prerequisite for tantric practice is some stable level of understanding of voidness — the absence of fantasized and impossible ways of existing — and dependent arising — the coming about of everything by depending on causes and circumstances. Everyone is capable of gaining employment because no one exists as a totally incompetent "loser," and finding a job depends on personal effort and the economic situation.

Some people dismiss tantric deity yoga as a form of self-hypnosis. Imagining we are already a Buddha, however, is not a form of self-deception. We each have the factors allowing us to achieve that goal — we all have "Buddha-nature." In other words, because each of us has a mind, a heart, communicative ability and physical energy, we possess all the raw materials needed to create the enlightening faculties of a Buddha. So long as we realize we are not yet actually at that stage, and do not inflate ourselves with illusions of grandeur, we can work with these Buddha-figures without psychological danger.

In tantra, then, we imagine we already possess the form, surroundings, abilities and enjoyments of a Buddha. The physical body of a Buddha is made of transparent clear light, capable of helping others tirelessly, and is never deficient in any way. Imagining ourselves as a Buddha-figure with boundless energy like this, however, does not render us a "workaholic" or a martyr incapable of saying no. Tantric practitioners of course take a rest when tired. Nevertheless, maintaining this type of self-image helps stretch our self-imposed limits. Everyone has an almost endless store of energy available to tap in emergencies. No one is too exhausted to rush to his or her child who has fallen and is hurt.

In addition, while practicing tantra, we feel that the environment around us is completely pure and conducive for everyone's progress. Imagining this does not mean ignoring ecological or social issues. However, to help others and ourselves overcome depression and feelings of despair, we stop dwelling on negative aspects. Sufficiently strong motivation and effective methods to transform our attitudes bring spiritual progress regardless of location. Rather than incessantly complaining and being a prophet of doom, we try to bring hope to ourselves and the world.

We also imagine we benefit others by acting as a Buddha does. We feel that by our very way of being, we effortlessly exert a positive enlightening influence on everyone around us. We can understand what this means if we have ever been in the presence of a great spiritual being, such as His Holiness the Dalai Lama or Mother Teresa. Most people, even if only slightly receptive, feel inspired and are moved to act in a more noble way. We imagine we have a similar effect on others. Our mere presence, or even mention of our names, calms others down, brings them peace of mind and joy, and stimulates them to achieve new heights.

Finally, we imagine we are able to enjoy things in the pure way a Buddha does. Our usual mode of enjoyment is mixed with confusion, often translated as "contaminated pleasure." We are always critical, never satisfied. We listen to music and cannot fully enjoy it because we keep thinking that the sound reproduction is not as good as it would be on our neighbor's equipment. A Buddha, however, delights in everything without even a trace of confusion. We imagine doing likewise, for example, when enjoying the offerings of light, incense, food and so on in the various rituals.

USING VISUALIZATION TO EXPAND OUR CAPACITIES

Many Buddha-figures have multiple physical features in an assortment of colors. Kalachakra, for example, has a rainbow of four faces and twenty-four arms. This might seem strange at first, but there are profound reasons for this. All the forms imagined in tantra have several purposes, and each of their parts and colors has many levels of symbolism. Their complexity reflects the nature of the goal of becoming a Buddha. Buddhas need to keep the full array of their realizations and qualities actively in mind, simultaneously, so as to use them effectively in helping others. Moreover, Buddhas need to be mindful of the myriad personal details of those they are helping so as always to do what is appropriate.

This is not an unreachable goal. We already keep many things in mind simultaneously. If we drive a car, for example, we are aware of our speed, the distance we need to stop or pass another vehicle, the speed and position of the cars around us, the rules of driving, the purpose and goal of our journey, the road signs and so on. At the same time, we coordinate our eyes, hands and feet, are alert to strange noises from the engine, and can even listen to music and hold a conversation. Tantric visualizations help to expand this ability.

Without some method, it is very difficult to train ourselves to keep in mind simultaneously twenty-four insights and qualities such as impermanence, compassion, patience and so forth. A verbal mnemonic device, such as a phrase made up of the initial letters of each item in the list, is helpful for remembering them in sequence. However, representing each insight and quality in a graphic form, such as the twenty-four arms of a Buddha-figure, makes it much easier to remain mindful of all of them at once. Consider the case of a teacher of a class of twenty-four children. For most people, it is quite difficult to keep the personalities and special needs of each child in mind when planning a lesson at home. Reviewing a list of their names may be somewhat helpful, but actually being in front of the class and seeing the pupils immediately and vividly brings to mind all the factors needed to modify the day's lesson.

A *mandala*, literally a symbolic universe, is a further aid in this process of expanding our mindfulness and seeing everything in a pure way. In this context, a mandala refers to the palace and its surrounding grounds in which a Buddha-figure lives. Like the parts of our body, each architectural feature corresponds to a realization or positive quality we need to keep actively in mind. As a palace, a mandala is actually a three-dimensional structure. A mandala made of colored powders or drawn on cloth is like an architect's blueprint of that building. During empowerments and subsequent meditational practice, no one visualizes the two-dimensional drawing, only the structure it represents.

GENERATION AND COMPLETE STAGE PRACTICE

Anuttarayoga tantra has two phases of practice. The first, the generation stage, involves complex visualizations. During daily meditation, we imagine a sequence of happenings which includes generating ourselves as one or more Buddha-figures inside the symbolic world of a mandala and bringing to mind an understanding or feeling of various points such as voidness and compassion. To help maintain the sequence, we usually read — or recite from memory — a *sadhana*, which is somewhat like a script for this daily opera of visualization.

The second phase of practice is the complete stage, sometimes translated as the "completion stage." As a result of efforts made during the previous step, everything is now complete for following the procedures that actually bring about the goal of becoming a Buddha. Having trained the power of imagination, we use it as the key to unlock our subtle energy system — the invisible channels and forces within our body that affect our moods and state of mind. Without practice of the previous generation stage, this system remains unavailable for meditative use. Once accessed, however, consciously moving subtle energies through its channels brings our clear light subtlest mind to the surface. Meditative work with this level of mind then creates the immediate causes for actually achieving the physical bodies and mind of a Buddha. The process is no longer one of imagination.

Success in tantra, as in everything in life, follows from the laws of cause and effect. Our ultimate goal is the fullest ability to benefit everyone. To accomplish this goal of a resultant tantra — an everlasting stream of bodies of a Buddha — we need to transform our basis tantra, the everlasting continuity of our primordial clear light mind. We need to make it function as a body of wisdom giving rise to a vast body of enlightening forms. This requires a pathway tantra, an everlasting stream of complete and generation stage practices. With the former, we access clear light mind through work with our subtle energy system, while with the latter we gain the tools for accomplishing that task by training our powers of concentration and imagination. Thus, each stage of tantric practice acts as the cause for attainment of its subsequent phase.

THE ROLE OF RECEIVING EMPOWERMENT AND TAKING VOWS

As part of our basis tantra, we each have the working materials from which to fashion the bodies of a Buddha. All the potentials we need are contained in our clear light mind — the principal aspect of our Buddha-nature, the main factor allowing each of us to become a Buddha. Before we can bring these potentials to fruition, however, we must activate them. This is the function and necessity of receiving empowerment. An initiation conferred by a fully qualified master first removes the initial obstacles that prevent access and use of these Buddha-potentials. It then awakens these abilities and reinforces them. This twofold procedure is called "receiving purification and planting seeds." The process only works, however, if we imagine or feel it is happening. Empowerment requires active participation by both the teacher and the disciple.

A spiritual master is vital to this process. Reading a ritual in a book or watching a video of it being performed is not powerful enough to activate Buddha-potentials. We need personally to participate in a live experience. This is not difficult to appreciate. We all know the difference between listening to a recording in our home and attending a live concert. Through personal exposure to a fully qualified master conferring empowerment, we gain inspiration, confidence, trust and a source of guidance to sustain all subsequent practice of tantra. Also, we establish a strong link not only with the teacher imparting the initiation, but with the entire lineage of masters through which the practice derives, tracing back to Buddha himself. Knowing that people have repeatedly achieved spiritual success through these techniques is very important psychologically and provides a great sense of confidence in the practice. Receiving empowerment, we are not embarking on some trivial undertaking. We are not fantasizing ourselves to be Mickey Mouse in Disneyland. We are joining a long line of serious practitioners who have validated the tantric techniques over centuries.

Without a trellis to grow on, a vine never rises from the ground. Similarly, a definite structure is essential for developing Buddha-potentials once they are activated. This is the purpose of the vows we make and the commitments we take at an anuttarayoga empowerment — they provide the necessary supporting structure for all subsequent progress. Tantric practice is not a casual hobby, nor is it limited to a meditation seat. The personal transformation we undertake with tantra encompasses every aspect of life. How can we proceed without clear guidelines? These guidelines are provided by the refuge commitments and the bodhisattva and tantric vows.

Taking refuge gives a safe and positive direction to life. We strive to remove our shortcomings and realize our potentials, as the Buddhas have done and highly realized practitioners are doing. With bodhisattva vows, we restrain ourselves from negative behavior contrary to that goal. We promise to refrain from acting in ways that damage our ability to help others. Keeping tantric vows ensures that we do not wander astray during the complexities of tantric practice. In short, it is a wondrous gift, not a constricting burden, that Buddha has imparted the guidelines of these vows and trainings. We do not have to learn by mistake which behavior to adopt or avoid in order to reach enlightenment for the benefit of all.

Receiving empowerment through an elegant ceremony provides a point of reference which we can look back upon as the beginning of our formal commitment to the tantric path. When we mark major transitions in life with age-old ritual, we take them far more seriously than we would if we just let them casually pass. Boarding the tantric vehicle and embarking on a more advanced phase of Buddhist practice is one such major transition. An empowerment, with its procedures for bonding with a tantric master and taking vows, marks this event in a memorable way.

COMMITMENT

Many people are frightened of making a commitment to anything — whether to a partner, a career or a spiritual path. Fearing that they will lose their freedom, they approach any commitment with indecision and hesitancy. Others feel that a commitment is a moral obligation, and if they break it, they are bad persons. Not wanting to make a wrong decision and risk being bad, they have difficulty taking any major step in life. Still others regard commitments as temporary and enter into them only if there is a clause for escape, such as obtaining a divorce. They make commitments lightly and break them easily as soon as they experience inconvenience.

Such attitudes, especially when applied toward committing ourselves to tantric practice, a spiritual master or keeping vows, are an obstacle to spiritual progress. A middle path is required. On the one hand, it is unwise to rush into anything before examining the consequences seriously. On the other hand, we need to take decisions in life, otherwise we never get anywhere. The way to overcome indecision is to evaluate honestly our capacity and readiness for making a commitment, to know clearly what we are committing ourselves to, and to understand deeply the relation between commitment and freedom. We need time and wisdom.

Corresponding to different levels of commitment, there are two ways of attending an initiation. We can come as either an active participant or an interested observer. Active participants take all the vows associated with the practice, try their best to do the visualizations and thus actually receive the empowerment. They subsequently model their lives in accordance with the guidelines of their vows and engage in at least the initial levels of tantric meditation. If we receive an anuttarayoga empowerment from the Gelug tradition, for example, we begin a daily meditative practice known as six-session yoga. Those who do not feel ready to take such a step attend as observers and do not actually receive the empowerment.

There is no shame or guilt involved with being an observer. It is far wiser to attend in this manner than to make a premature commitment we later regret. Interested observers, however, need not merely sit back and watch the ceremony as an entertaining anthropological spectacle. There is a great opportunity to gain much from the experience. Both participants and observers, then, find the initiation more meaningful when they understand beforehand the basic facts about tantra.

CHOOSING A TANTRA SYSTEM

Suppose we have a basic Buddhist outlook, a working foundation of insight, and a confident belief in the effectiveness and necessity for the anuttarayoga tantra techniques. If we feel we are ready to receive empowerment, or that we would like to attend one as an interested observer in order to make a strong connection for future involvement, the next question is which anuttarayoga system to choose? The menu is huge, in a foreign language, and most of us lack a close relationship with a spiritual teacher whom we could ask for advice. Sometimes, however, we do not have much choice since qualified masters seldom come to our local area and even more rarely confer an empowerment of this highest class.

The most important points to consider before taking an initiation are the qualifications of the teacher. Even if an unqualified person gives initiation into a tantra system we have strong interest to receive, it is of no use to attend. Anyone trained in ritual can recite and go through the motions of an initiation ceremony, but, lacking proper qualifications, a pretender confers nothing upon us. Even if the teacher is right, our choice of tantra systems is sometimes dictated by what others have requested and organized. Availability, however, is not the optimum criterion for choosing a tantra system of meditation. Sometimes our priority is to establish a close bond with the teacher, not necessarily the Buddha-figure for which he or she is conferring empowerment. Best, however, is to meet with both the right teacher and the right tantra system. To determine whether that system is Kalachakra, we need to know something about it.

CHAPTER TWO
Overview of Kalachakra

CYCLES OF TIME AND KARMA

The word *kalachakra* means cycles of time, and the Kalachakra system presents three such cycles — external, internal and alternative. The external and internal cycles deal with time as we normally know it, while the alternative cycles are practices for gaining liberation from these two. The structures of the external and internal cycles are analogous, similar to the parallel between macrocosm and microcosm discussed in Western philosophy. This means that the same laws that govern a universe also pertain to atoms, the body and our experience of life. The practices of the alternative cycles also follow this structure so as to allow us to engage with and surmount these forces in an efficient manner. Such mimicking is, in fact, one of the distinguishing features of the anuttarayoga tantra technique.

Time, in Buddhism, is defined as a measurement of change. For example, a month is the measurement of change involved either externally in the moon circling the earth or internally in a woman going from one menstruation to the next. Such changes are cyclical in that the pattern repeats, although the events of each cycle are not completely identical. Externally, the universe passes through cosmic, astronomical, astrological and historical cycles. On an internal level, the body goes through physiological cycles, many of which bring about associated mental and emotional cycles as well. Furthermore, just as universes form, expand, contract, disappear and then form once again, individual beings pass through continuing rebirths with repeated conception, growth, old age and death.

Normally the passage of time exercises a debilitating effect. As we age, our sight, hearing, memory and physical strength gradually weaken and eventually we die. Due to compulsive attachment and confusion about who we are and how we exist, we take rebirth without any control over its process or circumstances, each time having to relearn everything we knew before. As each of our lives unfolds over the course of time, karmic potentials from our previous actions ripen at appropriate astrological, historical and life-cycle moments into the various events we experience. Some of these are pleasant, but many are not. We seem to have little choice about what happens in life.

In short, the external and internal cycles of time delineate *samsara* — uncontrollably recurring rebirth, fraught with problems and difficulties. These cycles are driven by impulses of energy, known in the Kalachakra system as "winds of karma." *Karma* is a force intimately connected with mind and arises due to confusion about reality. Imagining that ourselves, others and everything around us exist in the way our mind makes them appear — as if with concrete, permanent identities established from within each being or thing — we act on the basis of this confusion with attachment, anger or stubborn foolishness. We think, for example, "I am definitely like this, those objects or persons are certainly like that, I must possess these things as mine and get rid of those that bother me," and so on. Any physical, verbal or mental action committed on the basis of such a rigid, confused way of thinking builds up karmic potentials and habits. Under appropriate circumstances, these potentials or "seeds of karma" ripen in the form of compelling impulses to repeat these acts, and to enter into situations in which similar actions happen to us. We can readily see this if we examine carefully the impulsive behavior behind the personal and historical events we experience. How many people blunder from one bad marriage to another, and how many countries from one crisis to the next?

Karmic potentials, in fact, give rise to a broad array of impulses that affect our lives. Collective karmic potentials from previous actions of a huge number of beings — including ourselves — give rise, for example, to the impulse for a universe to evolve with specific environments and life forms into which we and these beings subsequently take rebirth. These collective potentials also give rise to the impulses that drive the physical and biological laws that govern that universe — ranging from the weather patterns of its planets to the life-cycle habits of each species on them. They also account for the impulses behind the instinctive daily behavior characteristic of each life form.

Within this context, individual karmic potentials, at the appropriate juncture in each being's internal cycles — namely after each death — give rise to the impulse to take rebirth in a specific environment with a particular body. This impulse is relative to a particular evolutionary point in the external cycle of a universe. We cannot take rebirth as a dinosaur in a primeval forest when this life form and setting are already extinct. All these factors that ripen from karma work harmoniously together to provide the "container" within which we experience the ripening of other personal karmic potentials in the form of the impulsive behavior behind life's events. Born in a nation at war, we impulsively become a soldier, bomb enemy villages and one day are killed in battle. The many levels of external and internal cycles of time intertwine in a complex manner.

In short, time has neither beginning nor end. There has always been and will always be change, which can be labeled as the passage of time. Universes, civilizations and animate life forms continually arise and fall. The form they take depends on the actions, and therefore the minds of those who precede them. This is why there is a harmonious fit between the bodies and minds of beings and their environment. Someone is born as a fish to experience life's events in water or as a human in air, not vice versa. Because the minds of beings are under the influence of confusion, however, the bodies, mentalities and environments that result from the karmic actions they commit have a constricting, detrimental effect on them. These factors limit their abilities to benefit themselves and others. People living during the medieval plagues could do little to counter the horrors they faced.

LIBERATION FROM CYCLES OF TIME

The alternative cycles of time entail a graded series of meditative practices of anuttarayoga tantra. They serve not only as an alternative to the external and internal cycles, but as a way to gain liberation from them. The possibility of gaining liberation from time, however, does not imply that time does not actually exist or that someone can live and benefit others outside of time. Time, as a measurement of change, also occurs as a measure of the cycles of actions of a Buddha. Liberation from time means ridding ourselves of the confusion, and its instincts, that repeatedly give rise to the impulses, or karma, that render us at the mercy of the ravages of time. Once free, we are no longer adversely affected by external winter darkness, eclipses, wars and so on that periodically recur. Nor are we restricted by the type of body that is under the control of periodic biological forces, such as hunger, sexual urges, tiredness or aging. As a result of the full understanding of reality, it becomes possible, instead, to generate cycles of forms that benefit others beyond any limitations imposed by time.

The process begins with the Kalachakra initiation. Properly empowered, we engage in generation and then complete stage meditational practice in the form of the Buddha-figure called Kalachakra. Through these two stages, we access and utilize the subtlest level of our mind to see reality. Remaining continually focused on reality with it eliminates forever confusion and its instincts, thus bringing liberation from the external and internal cycles of time. This is possible because our basis tantra, our individual clear light mind, underlies each moment of experience and, like time, it has no end. Once our subtlest mind is freed from the deepest cause giving rise to the impulses of energy that perpetuate cycles of time and bondage to them, it gives rise, instead, to the bodies of a Buddha, in the form of Kalachakra.

THE SPREAD OF KALACHAKRA

In deciding whether to take the Kalachakra empowerment, it is helpful to know the origin of these teachings and the history of their spread. We then have confidence that its methods have been tested and proven effective over time.

According to tradition, Buddha taught the *Kalachakra Tantra* more than 2800 years ago in present-day Andhra Pradesh, southern India. The rulers of the northern land of Shambhala were the main audience and preserved these teachings in their country. In the tenth century, two Indian masters, in separate expeditions, attempted to reach Shambhala. On the way, each experienced a pure vision of that land in which he received transmission of the Kalachakra empowerment and corpus of material. Each spread these teachings in India, with only slight differences in their presentation. One of the last tantra systems to emerge historically, Kalachakra quickly achieved prominence and popularity in the monastic universities of the central Gangetic plain and then, shortly afterwards, in those of Kashmir. Four styles of practice eventually emerged. Masters from these areas taught Kalachakra in northern Burma, the Malay Peninsula and Indonesia, but it died out in these areas by the fourteenth century.

Together with Tibetan translators, Indian teachers also transmitted Kalachakra to Tibet. There were three primary transmissions between the eleventh and thirteenth centuries, with each lineage passing on a different blend of aspects from the four Indian versions and introducing further slight differences due to translation. Lineages, combining different components of these three transmissions, have passed down to the present through first the Sakya and Kagyü, and then also the Gelug traditions. Since the Nyingma school of Tibetan Buddhism transmits only Indian texts that reached Tibet and were translated prior to the early ninth century, there is no direct Nyingma lineage of Kalachakra. Later Nyingma masters, however, have received and conferred Kalachakra empowerment from other lineages, particularly that of the nineteenth-century Rimey or non-sectarian movement, and written commentaries on all aspects of the teachings. Moreover, there is a Kalachakra style of *dzogchen*, or great completeness practice.

Among the four Tibetan traditions, Kalachakra is most prominent within the Gelug. The study, practice and rituals of Kalachakra first received special attention in the fifteenth century at Tashilhünpo, the monastery of the early Dalai Lamas and later the Panchen Lamas in central Tibet. In the mid-seventeenth century it spread to what the Manchus soon called "Inner Mongolia," where the Mongols built the first monastic college dedicated specifically to Kalachakra. By the mid-eighteenth century there were Kalachakra colleges at the Manchu imperial court in Beijing, then Tashilhünpo, Amdo (northeastern Tibet) and so-called "Outer Mongolia." During the nineteenth century the Tibetans and the Mongols of Inner and Outer Mongolia transmitted

Kalachakra to the Buryat Mongols of Siberia and they, in turn, at the beginning of the twentieth century, spread it to the Kalmyk Mongols on the Volga River and the Siberian Turkic people of Tuva. As in other Mongol areas and Amdo, large sectors of the major monasteries of each of these regions devoted themselves to Kalachakra practice.

This enthusiasm of the Mongols, Amdo people and Tuvinians for Kalachakra is perhaps due to their identification of their countries with the fabled northern land of Shambhala. For more than a century many Russians also have embraced this belief as a result of their contact with the Buryats and Kalmyks. Madame Blavatsky and Nikolai Roerich, for example, gave Shambhala a prominent role in theosophy and agni yoga, the esoteric traditions each respectively founded. Agvan Dorjiev, the Thirteenth Dalai Lama's Buryat envoy to the Russian imperial court, convinced the last czar, Nikolai II, to sanction construction of a Kalachakra temple in St. Petersburg by explaining to him Russia's connection with Shambhala.

Kalachakra has also received prominent attention in the medical and astrological institutes of all four Tibetan Buddhist traditions within Tibet itself, Mongolia and other parts of Central Asia. This is because the calculations for compiling the Tibetan calendar and determining planetary positions, a large part of Tibetan astrology and a certain portion of Tibetan medical knowledge derive from the external and internal Kalachakra teachings. The Mongolian calendar, as well as astrological and medical systems, subsequently derived from the Tibetan ones. Kalachakra is thus the Buddhist equivalent of the "patron-saint" of these sciences.

KALACHAKRA AND THE LINE OF DALAI LAMAS

Many people wonder what is the connection between His Holiness the Dalai Lama and Kalachakra, and why does he give this initiation so often. His Holiness modestly claims there is no special relation between the line of Dalai Lamas and Kalachakra, despite the Dalai Lamas being considered incarnations of one of the Shambhala rulers. Nevertheless, the First, Second, Seventh, Eighth and the present Fourteenth Dalai Lamas have taken strong interest in the Kalachakra system. Since the time of the Seventh Dalai Lama in the early eighteenth century, Kalachakra ritual and meditational practices have been specialities of the Namgyal Monastery, the personal monastery of the Dalai Lamas at the Potala Palace in Lhasa.

There is no restriction on the number of times the Kalachakra empowerment may be given during the lifetime of a master and there is no special reason why His Holiness the present Dalai Lama confers it so frequently. His Holiness has said he is happy to give it when requested, provided the circumstances are conducive. Since 1970, he has conferred the empowerment in numerous places in India, as well as in North America, Europe, Mongolia and Australia. Several other great masters of the Gelug, Kagyü, Sakya and Nyingma traditions have conferred it widely as well. It makes little difference from which lineage the Kalachakra initiation is received. They all empower us to study and practice the vast array of its teachings.

KALACHAKRA AND WORLD PEACE

We always hear that the Kalachakra empowerment is for world peace. Some people even choose Kalachakra over other anuttarayoga tantra systems because of this association. But what exactly is the connection between Kalachakra and peace, and why do so many people attend? Although empowerments for other tantras are intended for only a small number of disciples at a time, there is a historical tradition of conferring the Kalachakra initiation to large crowds of people. Buddha first gave it to the king of Shambhala and his entourage of ninety-six minor rulers. In time, their descendants conferred it upon the entire population of Shambhala in order to unite them against the threat of a possible invasion and avert annihilation. This is the origin of the association of the Kalachakra empowerment with world peace and the tradition of conferring it upon large numbers of participants.

According to the Kalachakra presentation of historical cycles, barbaric hordes periodically invade the civilized world and try to eliminate all possibilities for spiritual practice. A future invasion is predicted for the year 2424 of this common era, when it is said there will be another brutal world war. At that time help will come from Shambhala to defeat the barbarians. A new golden age will dawn, with everything conducive for spiritual practice, particularly of Kalachakra. All those who have previously received the Kalachakra initiation will be reborn at that time on the victorious side. The highest motivation for receiving the empowerment is to be able to practice the Kalachakra methods now in order to achieve enlightenment in this very lifetime. Nevertheless, people have traditionally flocked to the initiation with the motivation of planting karmic seeds to connect themselves with this future golden age so as to complete its practice then.

SHAMBHALA

Since Shambhala plays a prominent role in the Kalachakra system, most people are curious to know what Shambhala actually is and where it is located. It is undoubtedly from a distortion of the name "Shambhala" that the Western romantic writer James Hilton has derived the myth of Shangri-la — a hidden paradise on Earth. Although there may be a place in this world representative of Shambhala, that is not the actual fabled land. Shambhala cannot be found on this planet or even in some distant world. It is, however, a human realm in which everything is conducive for spiritual practice, particularly of Kalachakra.

Meditational masters have written guidebooks, in both Sanskrit and Tibetan, for reaching Shambhala. They describe the journey as a physical one only up to a certain point. The sojourner must subsequently repeat millions of mantras and other special practices in order to arrive at the final goal. The journey to Shambhala, then, is primarily a spiritual one. The aim of receiving Kalachakra initiation is not to reach or be reborn in Shambhala, but, like all other mahayana, or "vast vehicle" Buddhist practices, is to gain enlightenment here and now for the benefit of all. The empowerment plants the seeds enabling us to reach this goal and helps purify some of the grosser internal obstacles that would prevent its attainment.

ASSESSING OUR PREPARATION FOR RECEIVING EMPOWERMENT

Suppose we develop interest in Kalachakra based on knowing something about the special contents of its teachings, its history and relation to world peace. We still need to decide whether we are actually ready to receive empowerment and embark on its practice, or whether it is better to attend as a well-informed and admiring observer. The most reasonable course is to base our decision on how well prepared we are. Although hundreds of thousands of prostrations, repetitions of the hundred-syllable Vajrasattva mantra and so forth are extremely helpful, the main preparation is training in *lamrim* — the graded pathways of behaving, communicating, thinking and feeling that lead to enlightenment.

The first step is to take the safe, sound and positive direction in life indicated by the Buddhas, their teachings and the community of those well-advanced in that direction. Usually translated as "taking refuge," this is the direction of working on ourselves to overcome problems and gain the qualities necessary for benefiting others as fully as possible. Putting this direction in life means leading our life on the basis of understanding and confidence in the laws of behavioral cause and effect. To avoid suffering and problems, we refrain from acting destructively, and to experience happiness, we act in a constructive manner.

The most important preparation for tantra is striving to develop the three principal pathway attitudes, or outlooks on life: renunciation, bodhichitta and the understanding of voidness. Renunciation is the willingness to give up problems and their causes, and is based on a strong determination to be free from the suffering they engender. For example, because we are totally disgusted with being lonely and frustrated, we are willing and determined to give up not only our unhealthy relationships with others, but also our negative personality traits and confused, distorted self-image which make our relations non-fulfilling. Bodhichitta is a heart that is set on achieving enlightenment — overcoming all shortcomings and realizing all potentials — for everyone's sake. It is motivated by love and compassion for all beings, and a sense of responsibility to help them as much as possible to overcome their problems and attain lasting happiness. Voidness means an absence of fantasized ways of existing.

Normally, we imagine ourselves, others and all phenomena to exist in impossible ways that do not accord with reality. We mentally fabricate fantasies of varying levels of subtlety and project them onto ourselves and onto everything and everyone around us. For example, on one level we imagine we are born to lose, we can never succeed in establishing or maintaining a satisfying relation with anyone, and that the other person or external circumstances are never at fault when things go wrong. On a more subtle level, we are preoccupied with ourselves, thinking we exist as some solid "me" inside our head whom we fear no one will like and everyone will reject. Confusing these fantasies with reality, we act out of ignorance and the insecurity it generates. Even before any conflict arises, we are so nervous and self-conscious that we ensure the relationship fails. Our behavior not only builds up and reinforces a pattern of karmic potentials for problems to ripen in future relationships, but also triggers the ripening of past potentials in the form of present rejections.

Before entering tantric practice, we need to understand that at least the grossest levels of our projections do not refer to anything real. No one is a born loser and no relation is doomed to failure. Such understanding comes from an outlook on reality, or "correct view" of voidness, corresponding to at least one of the mahayana systems of philosophical tenets Buddha taught — chittamatra or one of the several madhyamaka ones. According to these systems, not only ourselves, but everything is devoid of existing in fantasized ways. The particular systems differ primarily according to the level of subtlety of fantasy they address.

As further preparation for tantra, faith and confidence are needed in the tantric methods in general, and particularly in those of its highest class, anuttarayoga, as constituting the most efficient and effective means for attaining enlightenment. Anyone having this confident belief, the frame of mind of the three principal paths and a background in lamrim is called a "proper vessel" for receiving the Kalachakra empowerment. We must judge for ourselves if we are sufficiently prepared.

OVERVIEW OF THE INITIATION

The initiation process spans several days, with the first day being a preparation ceremony, followed by usually two or three days of actual empowerment. The most important part of the initial procedures is taking refuge and the bodhisattva and tantric vows. Without all three, we cannot actually receive empowerment, although we may witness it and derive great benefit. The empowerment itself involves a complex procedure of imagining ourselves transforming into a series of special forms, entering the mandala of the Buddha-figure Kalachakra, and experiencing in it a sequence of purifications and the awakening and enhancing of potentials for future success in the practice. The mandala is an enormous multi-storied palace, in and around which are 722 figures, including a principal couple in the center. The master conferring the empowerment simultaneously appears as all these figures, not just as the central one. Thus, throughout the process we visualize ourselves, our teacher and our surroundings in a very special way.

The steps of the initiation are extremely intricate and, without familiarity, the visualizations involved can be quite perplexing. But if, as a proper vessel, we take the vows with full sincerity and at least feel, with strong faith, that all the visualizations are actually occurring, we can be confident that we are receiving the empowerment. With this basis secured, the next step is seeking further instruction and then trying, as sincerely as possible, to travel the full path to enlightenment as presented in the *Kalachakra Tantra*.

CHAPTER THREE
External Kalachakra

KALACHAKRA: THE CLEAR TANTRA

Let us look briefly at some of the vast material in the *Kalachakra Tantra* itself. It is not necessary to study this material in depth in order to take the empowerment or attend as an observer. Nevertheless, some acquaintance with it helps to develop an appreciation of the wide range of topics included in the Kalachakra teachings and a respect for their value. This ancient text contains a great deal of practical advice for people and societies that is still relevant today. It is a veritable encyclopedia of not only sophisticated techniques for attaining enlightenment, but also thought-provoking social commentary and scientific analysis.

Kalachakra is called the clear tantra, while the other anuttarayoga tantras are known as obscure. The main reason for this differentiation concerns the fourth initiation, which empowers us to perceive simultaneously and straightforwardly the two levels of truth concerning reality. The Kalachakra system formulates the two truths as clear light mind generated as an unchanging blissful awareness of the voidness of everything, and the appearances to which such a mind gives rise. In other anuttarayoga systems, the words of this stage of empowerment do not explain the unity of the two levels directly, just by analogy. The Kalachakra empowerment, on the other hand, explains this union explicitly. In fact, although Kalachakra differs significantly from the other anuttarayoga systems on many points, studying Kalachakra often clarifies enigmatic points of texts from those systems. Furthermore, the entire *Kalachakra Tantra* is written in clear language, unlike the other tantras which require an elaborate scheme to decode the many levels of meaning hidden behind their terse, poetic style.

THE TEXTUAL TRADITION

How was the *Kalachakra Tantra* actually written? According to tradition, Suchandra, the King of Shambhala was the main disciple for the first Kalachakra empowerment. He subsequently wrote down in verse, in his own language, the *Root Kalachakra Tantra* and an extensive commentary to it. Interestingly, a grammarian assisted him who purposely made several mistakes in the meter and count of the verses. He did this in order to help the King and the people of that time to overcome attachment to regularity and rigid forms. Although the Kalachakra material, with its external, internal and alternative cycles, abounds with symmetry, it is important not to be a slave to order and expect that everything in the universe be neat and regular, or that we can always be in control. As one of my Tibetan mentors, Sharpa Rinpochey, once said, "Symmetry is stupid." Although many things in this world are indeed analogous to each other, if we insist that everything is inherently symmetrical and therefore controllable, we are living in a fantasy of false expectation. Just because there are five of this, does not necessarily mean there are five of that. Unexpected exceptions always occur.

Suchandra was followed by six generations of kings before Manjushri-yashas inherited the Shambhala throne, becoming the first of a line of twenty-five *Kalki* rulers, or Keepers of the Caste. He composed the *Abridged Kalachakra Tantra*, while his son and successor, Pundarika, wrote a commentary to it, *Stainless Light*. These are the two basic Kalachakra texts that the visionaries Chilupa and Kalachakrapada the Elder transmitted to India and which survive today. Each contains five chapters. The first two chapters concern the external and internal cycles of time, respectively, while the last three present the alternative cycles. The third chapter discusses the empowerment, the fourth the generation stage and the fifth the complete stage and the attainment of enlightenment. All later commentaries follow this five-part structure. Let us survey the contents of these chapters in the wider context of the rich Sanskrit and Tibetan Kalachakra literature.

DESCRIPTION OF THE UNIVERSE

The first chapter of the *Abridged Kalachakra Tantra* begins by explaining the method of condensing the *Root Tantra*, and presents the outline of that monumental opus. The text then sets the stage by telling how Buddha first gave the empowerment to King Suchandra and how the King brought the teachings back to Shambhala. To locate Shambhala requires the study of geography. The context for that is the discussion of the universe, which follows next in most of the commentaries.

The Kalachakra description of the universe is quite different from that presented in the other major Buddhist system of metaphysics: *abhidharma*, or topics of special knowledge. There are, of course, common elements in both, found in non-Buddhist Indian descriptions as well. These include multiple universes each passing through, at different times from each other, beginningless four-part cycles of formation, stabilization, disintegration and being empty, and each universe having a core mountain, Mount Meru, surrounded by continents, heavens and hells. The main differences between the two Buddhist systems concern the specifics of the four-part cycles, and the shape and size of the universe, Mount Meru and the continents.

It is significant that Buddhism offers two descriptions of the universe. Each is valid for a different purpose, and in neither case is that purpose navigating a ship. This allows for the modern scientific depiction to be perfectly acceptable in Buddhism as valid for the purpose of travel, and there being no contradiction in having multiple portraits. The description of any phenomenon, then, is dependent on not only the conceptual framework of the author and the audience, but also the use to which that description is put. We would certainly explain the plans to send a manned mission to Mars in a different manner to the politicians who are deciding the budget than to the engineers who are designing the machinery. Both portrayals of the mission, however, are valid, useful and necessary. Appreciating this point helps us understand voidness. Nothing exists with inherent characteristics on its own side rendering only one correct way to conventionally perceive, apprehend or describe it.

The purpose of the abhidharma picture of the universe is to help practitioners develop discriminating awareness by working with complex systems of multiple variables. The purpose of the Kalachakra version is quite different. It is to provide the Buddhist equivalent of a unified field theory that explains the structure and workings of the cosmos, atoms, the human body and the experience of rebirth in a parallel manner. The need for this unified theory is to provide a comprehensive basis, covering as much of samsara as possible, at which to aim the meditative practices of alternative Kalachakra for gaining liberation and enlightenment.

A description of the external and internal worlds in terms of their unifying parallels reveals the shared underlying basis from which both derive — namely, clear light mind. The winds of karma that provide the impulses for a particular universe to evolve come from the collective karma on the clear light minds of prior beings. These clear light minds remain present during empty eons in between universal epochs. Likewise, the winds of karma that provide the impulses for a specific rebirth to occur arise from the individual karma on the clear light mind of a particular being. That clear light mind also continues during bardo periods in between rebirths.

Meditation in analogy with the cycles through which the external and internal worlds pass — and, in particular, in analogy with how each of these cycles periodically returns to its clear light basis — provides a means to reach that basis. This is a unique feature of the anuttarayoga tantra technique. Once clear light mind is accessed, it is possible to make the necessary changes — namely, by focusing on voidness, to eliminate the confusion and its instincts that cloud it — so that this basis no longer gives rise to the problems and sufferings associated with the external and internal cycles. This is the deepest reason why the proportions and shape of the universe, human body, and the mandala and body of the Buddha-figure Kalachakra are all the same.

SPACE PARTICLES AND THE ORIGINS OF A UNIVERSE

One of the most interesting points from the Kalachakra description of the universe is its description of space particles. The *Kalachakra Tantra* speaks a great deal about atomic particles and the six elements — earth, water, fire, wind, space and consciousness or deep awareness. This last element is not physical and corresponds to primordial clear light mind, the basis from which the other, grosser elements manifest and on which they rest. Corresponding to the five grosser elements are five types of atomic or subatomic particles — earth particles, water particles and so on — each more subtle than the last. The most subtle are space particles which constitute the smallest building blocks of matter. When the four grosser particles are manifest, space particles are the space between them.

In Kalachakra, these space particles are intimately linked to the origins of a universe. This presentation has aroused the interest of scientists, as it suggests certain points that can be related to modern ideas about the structure of the universe. All universes are made of atomic particles. According to current scientific theory, the universe starts with a big bang, expands by means of particles and atoms becoming increasingly complex and compounding together, and then contracts and ends with a big crunch. Similarly, Kalachakra describes eons of formation in which atomic particles also join together, followed by eons of endurance and eons of disintegration.

What is of particular interest is the period in between these cycles. Buddhism calls these periods "empty eons," while the closest equivalent in modern science is the period in which a galaxy contracts into a black hole. According to the abhidharma description, during empty eons the basic elements exist merely in potential form. The Kalachakra teachings, however, say that in this period only a space particle exists. In this context, a space particle consists of a trace of the grosser elemental particles of a universe which are no longer joined together. In scientific terms, this is a situation in which the ordinary laws of physics do not operate, as is the case with black holes.

An empty eon ends when, by the force of winds of karma from the actions of animate beings of previous eons, an impulse occurs for the subatomic particles once more to coagulate and for ordinary physical laws to take over again. Thus the space particle of a particular universe during its empty eon is somewhat like a super-condensed kernel of its matter from which its next phase of expansion grows. This depiction is especially interesting in light of the recent discovery that a black hole emits radiation as matter collapses into it, and suggests a correlation between the life-cycle of galaxies and of the universe in general. Even more intriguing is that the internal Kalachakra teachings elaborate a parallel process which operates during each person's experience of death and rebirth.

THE LOCATION OF SHAMBHALA
Just as modern science describes galaxies and the universe in general as having a center around which everything revolves, Kalachakra also portrays each universe as having an axis, but in the form of a mountain,

called Meru. The continents do not actually revolve around this core mountain, but encircle it, remaining stationary while the sun, moon, planets and stars rotate overhead. The land mass is divided into twelve continents, paralleling the division of the ecliptic into the twelve signs of the zodiac. The ecliptic is the band in the sky through which the sun, moon and planets course. The northern half of the southern continent is divided into six regions, like horizontal bands. India is the southernmost, while Shambhala is the fifth.

The first chapter later presents the calculations for the length of the shortest day of winter in these six regions. Based on these, Shambhala can be identified with the region surrounding Mount Kailash, the mountain in southwestern Tibet holy to both Hindus and Buddhists. This makes sense because, according to Tibetan etymology, *Shambhala* means the abode of bliss, a synonym for both the Hindu god Shiva and the Buddha-figure Heruka. Hinduism regards Mount Kailash as the seat of Shiva, and Buddhism as the main location of Heruka. Some scholars identify the three regions between India and Shambhala — Bhotia, Li and Chin — as Tibet, Khotan and China, and then presume that Shambhala is somewhere in East Turkistan (the modern Chinese province of Xinjiang), but this seems to be erroneous. These three names are also used respectively for the Terai, Kathmandu Valley and Dolpo regions of southern, central and northwestern Nepal. The sixth region, Himavan, the land of snows, is a common name for Tibet.

Mount Kailash is not really Shambhala, however, but only represents Shambhala on this earth. The *Kalachakra Tantra* speaks of four holy places around Vajrasana (Bodh Gaya), the site where Buddha manifested his enlightenment: Five-peaked Mountain in the east, Potala Mountain in the south, Shambhala in the north and Oddiyana in the west. These are the special places associated, respectively, with Manjushri, Avalokiteshvara, the Kalki rulers and Guru Rinpochey. They can be identified with Wutaishan in northern China, the Vindhya Range in southern India, Mount Kailash in southwestern Tibet and Swat in northern Pakistan. If we go to these places, however, we do not actually find these great beings living there, or even archeological traces of them. As explained earlier, the journey to Shambhala is a spiritual, not a physical one.

THE THREAT OF INVASION

The first chapter continues with a discussion of the history of Shambhala and particularly the times of the first Kalki ruler, Manjushri-yashas, in which the threat of invasion by a barbaric horde loomed over the land. Although the Kalachakra teachings had been present in Shambhala for seven centuries, they were primarily studied and practiced at the royal court. Most of the people were Hindus, but the pure principles of Hinduism had greatly declined. Caste differences were extremely rigid and the society was not harmonious. The King saw that if his people remained strongly divided, with certain groups unwilling to eat with or even associate with each other, there would be no way to resist the invasion. Therefore he decided to unite all the castes into one by making everyone "vajra brothers and sisters." He accomplished this by gathering the entire population into the huge Kalachakra mandala palace his ancestors had built in the royal park, and conferring empowerment on those who wished to participate. The rest observed.

The King's intention was not to convert everyone to Buddhism. Rather, he explained that each religion teaches the same basic moral principles, but when people do not follow their religions purely, they fall from these principles. By joining everyone into one caste in the Kalachakra mandala, he called upon his people to return to the pure teachings of their own religions. Only with such a basis could they best face a demoralizing threat to their society. The King's call for unity and peace through Kalachakra initiation is still relevant today. Observers of a Kalachakra empowerment are not asked to forsake their native religions, but to live up to their ideals and unite in brotherhood and sisterhood with others doing likewise.

BARBARIC HORDES

Some scholars identify the barbarians mentioned in the Kalachakra literature as Muslims, but this is a hasty and irresponsible conclusion. The Sanskrit word for barbarian, *mleccha*, means anyone who speaks a non-Sanskrit language, eats beef, and behaves coarsely and crudely. Indians have used this term to label all invaders, starting from Alexander the Great. If we examine world history, invasions by barbaric forces inimical to spiritual freedom seem indeed to be cyclical. Although the Kalachakra literature describes many features of the barbarians that suggest they were Islamic — such as their tradition being founded in Mecca, being centered in Baghdad, men being circumcised, women wearing veils, special religious methods for slaughtering cattle, and so on — it does not seem that Islam in general is the reference.

During the early Abassid Caliphate, specifically during the second half of the eighth century and the start of the ninth, fanatic terrorist groups attacked the orthodox Sunni Muslim rulers in Baghdad, Samarqand and elsewhere, trying to overthrow the dynasty. These terrorists followed a religion which they called Islam, but which was actually a cult that adulterated the pure teachings of the *Qur'an* with many other doctrines, including those of Manichaeism, another religion of the time. The fact that the Kalachakra literature records the list of prophets of the barbarians as including not only Adam, Moses, Jesus, Mohammed and the future messiah Mahdi, but also Mani, the founder of Manichaeism, suggests that the barbarians were in fact some of these terrorist groups. After their defeat, many of them migrated to present-day northern Afghanistan where they encountered a multi-religious society of Buddhists, Hindus, Zoroastrians and Muslims. Their coming would certainly have been seen as a potential invasion of barbarians, and the call for everyone to join together in harmony and follow purely the ethical principles of their own religions would have been made to the local Muslims as well. This is an important point to remember in our present world. Each religion has its fanatic, fundamentalist, terrorist element. We must always take care not to confuse the policies of these disruptive small groups with the pure, original teachings of their mother religions.

The Buddhist solution to barbaric terrorism and violence is for society to face them with ethical solidarity. This approach is not unique to Buddhism. Nowadays many religious and political leaders around the globe call for a return to basic moral values. King Manjushri-yashas advised his people to examine their customs and those of the barbarians. If they found them similar, then their children and grandchildren would see no great difference between the ways of their forefathers and the barbarians. That being the case, they would more easily accept barbarian rule. The belief of Manjushri-yashas was that if we immediately resort to violence in dealing with all threats to ourselves and our society, we are no different from savage barbarians. We must seek peaceful solutions.

LEVELS OF MEANING OF SHAMBHALA

From the above discussion, we can see that from a modern historian's point of view, Shambhala is most likely in what is now northern Afghanistan. The fact that major Buddhist monasteries in this area followed the pre-Islamic Iranian court custom of depicting the twelve signs of the zodiac around the ceiling of their main halls adds further support for this hypothesis. Figures representing the twelve zodiac signs also surround the Kalachakra mandala. Thus just as different purposes call for distinct descriptions of the universe, the same is true concerning Shambhala. For explaining the calculations for the length of the shortest day of the year, Shambhala is the Mount Kailash area. For the sake of explaining historical cycles of invasions, it is northern Afghanistan. For the sake of a spiritual goal, it is a state of mind that can be reached only by intensive meditational practice. Shambhala, then, is simply a name given to various places relative to specific needs. Upon ultimate scrutiny, Shambhala cannot be found.

The relevancy of understanding this point is that it eliminates suspicion about the origin and validity of the Kalachakra practices. Traditionally it is said that Buddha taught Kalachakra 2800 years ago and that it was preserved in Shambhala and reintroduced into India through a transmission received in a vision. To most modern people this sounds rather incredible and they naturally doubt whether Kalachakra is an authentic teaching of the Buddha.

Dharmakirti, a seventh-century Indian Buddhist master, has explained that if a teaching is consistent with what Buddha has expounded and is effective for achieving its stated goal of liberation or enlightenment, then we can say that its source is Buddha's omniscient mind, whether or not the historical Buddha actually delivered it. Thus, for the purpose of gaining confidence in omniscient mind, we can label the source of the Kalachakra teachings as Buddha and Shambhala. For the purpose of historical analysis, we can postulate its source as the Buddhist monasteries of ninth-century northern Afghanistan. From the point of view of voidness and dependent arising, there is no contradiction. Since the Kalachakra teachings are consistent with other systems Buddha taught, and their practice certainly seems to bring about their intended results, as evidenced by His Holiness the Dalai Lama and other great contemporary Kalachakra masters, we can rest assured that the empowerment is the entrance to a reliable spiritual path.

THE USE OF HINDU IMAGES

In order to unite his people, King Manjushri-yashas followed Buddha's example by using the language and metaphors of the audience he taught. Since the majority of his subjects were Hindu, he freely borrowed Hindu images, concepts and terminology. He styled himself and his descendants as Kalki rulers. Kalki is the tenth and final *avatar* or incarnation of the Hindu god Vishnu who will come in the future as a messiah to fight in an apocalyptic war. In the Hindu *purana* literature, Kalki will be born in Shambhala, located in the mountains of present-day northern Uttar Pradesh, India. Perhaps Manjushri-yashas just borrowed the name Shambhala to refer to his kingdom and it was never actually called by that name. It hardly matters. The important point is that for achieving peaceful cooperation among people of different cultures and religions, it is unwise to try to force everyone to speak our own language, use our own cultural metaphors and convert to our own religion or political philosophy. The way to encourage others to be open-minded and receptive to the message of peace is to appeal to the specific aspects of their own culture, religion and political philosophy that naturally resonate with this aim.

THE PROPHESY OF A FUTURE WORLD WAR

King Manjushri-yashas prophesied another barbaric invasion for the year 2424, when anti-spiritual forces will wage a galactic war of conquest and destruction not limited to this planet. He advised the people of that future era to unite in the same way as his own subjects. He also predicted that forces from Shambhala, led by the twenty-fifth Kalki ruler, would arrive at that time in flying ships to turn the tide of battle and defeat the invading hordes. On the basis of this prophesy, some people have proposed that Shambhala is somewhere in outer space and that its inhabitants travel in flying saucers. As supporting evidence they cite the belief of the Aymara Indians of Bolivia and the Zulus of South Africa that several millennia ago extraterrestrial beings brought the science of calendar-making and other technological skills to this planet. We must take care, however, not to jump to hasty conclusions. Although Buddhism accepts the presence of intelligent life in other parts of the universe, as soon as we open the door for outer space heroes to soar in on flying saucers, we also open the door for witches to fly in on broomsticks.

The Kalachakra commentaries explain that wars against spirituality must be understood on two levels: as invasions by external hordes of barbarians, and as attacks by internal swarms of barbaric disturbing emotions and attitudes, led by confusion about reality. The various weapons and forces mentioned by the King that need to be used to win victory symbolize various realizations gained through spiritual practice, such as compassion, clear seeing of reality and so forth. These forces have their home in clear light mind which, like the etymological meaning of Shambhala, is the abode of bliss.

The fifteenth-century Gelug commentator Kaydrubjey has cautioned not to consider these wars on only a symbolic level, and to remember that they also refer to historical events. The external, internal and alternative cycles of time are all equally real. The closest example in Western culture is the account of exodus in the *Old Testament*. In the mystical tradition of Judaism, exodus symbolizes the spiritual path. Born into the slavery of confusion, we first must free ourselves from its grossest bonds and then wander in the desert of further spiritual practice until finding the promised land. This symbolism is based on a historical occurrence and its application as an analogy does not question that the event actually happened. The same is true of the prophesied war of the future.

PREVENTING WAR THROUGH SHARING TECHNOLOGY

How best to handle a threat of war? King Manjushri-yashas advised that sharing the achievements of our culture could turn invaders from their barbaric ways without resorting to battle. If others can appreciate the advantages offered by a more refined way of life, and have its advances made readily available to them, they may shed their violent methods more easily. The King used the example of sharing the scientific and technological knowledge of Shambhala with the barbarians and warned against keeping this knowledge secret. The King's wise counsel is still relevant today. Universal education and equal opportunity for self-improvement are the most potent methods for preventing violent crime.

At the time of King Manjushri-yashas, tables of planetary positions were compiled and circulated so that people did not have to work out the complicated mathematics themselves. In some societies at the time, however, this was done with the intention that the public would soon lose the skill and ability to make the calculations themselves. On one level, this would force people to rely on the *pandits*, the so-called "experts," who could exploit their ignorance for economic gain and social status. On another level, it would render the public open to deception because those who circulated these tables could easily tamper with them.

Leaders in those days planned uprisings and attacks on the basis of auspicious astrological signs. Strategy based on planetary positions given in fraudulent official tables would be incorrect and no one would have the knowledge to check or correct them. To avoid such exploitation, it was essential for the mathematics to be kept widely available for anyone to learn. It is for such reasons that the first chapter of the *Kalachakra Tantra* presents the mathematics for calculating the position of the planets, the timings of eclipses and for creating a lunar calendar correlated with a solar year.

We face similar dangers nowadays if people become so dependent on calculators and computers that they are no longer able to do simple arithmetic. And if we recall how difficult it is to correct computer errors with our telephone bills or credit ratings, we can appreciate the necessity for public knowledge of how to redress misinformation.

Just as the Kalachakra and modern scientific descriptions of the universe are not equivalent since each serves a different purpose, likewise the positions of the planets derived from each do not correspond to one another. The main purpose of Kalachakra astronomy and calendar-making is not to make interstellar navigational guidance systems, but to gain astrological information Thus King Manjushri-yashas explained that if we are forced to fight a war, we need astrological means to determine the best times to start campaigns and attacks. This is true whether the battle is external or internal. In this context, the first chapter of the *Kalachakra Tantra* presents an elaborate body of astrological calculations and teachings. This forms the basis for a large part of the Tibeto-Mongolian system of astrology, which derives the rest of its material from the Chinese tradition.

KARMA AND ASTROLOGY

Since the alternative cycles of time are methods for liberating ourselves from the domination of the external and internal cycles — from being under the control of karma — it is essential to understand clearly the relation between karma and astrology. Otherwise, astrology may simply increase superstition. At the time of King Manjushri-yashas astrological superstition led to the widespread custom of sacrificing animals and even humans to the sun in order to gain good fortune. Therefore the King emphasized that heavenly bodies do not cause events to occur in life. From the Buddhist perspective, no event is fixed or predetermined, otherwise liberation and enlightenment would be impossible.

Every person is born with an enormous array of karmic potentials built up over beginningless lifetimes. A natal chart and the predictions based on it are only indicative of a dominant karmic pattern with which we are born. There are many other possibilities as well. Moreover, an astrological chart only deals with a limited number of variables, whereas karma is infinitely more complex. As Kaydrubjey has said, if a natal chart indicated everything, then a man and a dog born at the same time in the same place would have the same personalities and experiences. Similarly, if an auspicious day were favorable for everyone, no one would be injured or killed in an accident that day anywhere in the world. Astrological configurations merely provide possible circumstances for appropriate karmic potentials to ripen. Without those potentials, nothing special happens, and even with them, sometimes further circumstances are necessary for their ripening.

KALACHAKRA ASTROLOGY

Keeping these points in mind, let us briefly survey the Kalachakra astrological material. Like other Indian systems, Kalachakra shares certain features with ancient Greek astrology. These include the twelve signs of the zodiac and their names, a seven-day week with days named after the heavenly bodies, and discussion of the sun, the moon and the planets Mercury, Venus, Mars, Jupiter and Saturn.

The *Kalachakra Tantra* also discusses the north and south nodes of the moon, which it presents as planets. These nodes are called Rahu and Ketu in Hindu astrology, and Rahu and Kalagni in the Kalachakra system. Although the sun and moon both course through the band of the sky called the ecliptic, their orbits do not exactly coincide. Their intersection points are the north and south nodes of the moon. When, on a new moon, the sun and moon are both at one of these points in the sky, there is a lunar eclipse. When, on a full moon, the sun and moon are on the opposing points, there is a solar eclipse. The symbolism of eclipse is a major theme that repeats in the internal and alternative cycles of time.

As with descriptions of the universe and calculations of planetary positions, astrological systems also differ according to their purpose. Western astrology analyzes the personality based on a natal chart — the position of the planets relative to the exact time and location of a person's birth. It predicts a person's future experiences by comparing these natal positions with where the heavenly bodies are located at different points in his or her life. Hindu systems also calculate a natal chart, but emphasize the unfolding of a person's life through periods ruled by successive planets. Kalachakra shares the Hindu orientation and features, but stresses predictive astrology based on using the calendar itself along with extensive almanac information.

TECHNIQUES FOR PREDICTING THE FUTURE

Kalachakra astrology employs two main systems for making predictions. The first divides the ecliptic into twenty-seven constellations rather than the twelve that constitute the more common zodiac. It assigns one of four elements — earth, water, fire, and air or wind — to each constellation and each of the seven days of the week. Comparing the element of the day of the week with the element of the constellation the moon is in at a specific time during that day, it interprets the combination to determine the auspiciousness of the moment for starting an undertaking such as a field battle, meditative retreat or monastic life.

The second system is called "arising from vowels." The Sanskrit alphabet has five families of vowels: *a, i,* vocalic *r, u* and vocalic *l.* These are correlated to the five elements, respectively, of space, wind, fire, water and earth. Associated with the vowel of each family are a diphthong and semivowel, for example *e* and *ya* with *i,* and all of these have lengthened forms, such as *ī, ai* and *yā.* The system assigns the resulting thirty vowels, one each, to the thirty dates of a lunar month. Someone wishing advice about the outcome of an undertaking consults an astrologer who compares the element of the first vowel of the client's name with the element of the vowel assigned to the date on which he or she asks the question. The system also assigns an element to each direction. Thus an astrologer can employ similar methods to determine the best direction from which a specific general should attack on a particular auspicious date, or from which a meditator should approach a ritual fire for making burnt offerings at the conclusion of a retreat.

The presentation of the "arising from vowels" system leads to a full phonemic analysis of the Sanskrit alphabet, with each letter assigned one of the five elements. This system has a counterpart in the internal cycles of time, but plays an especially prominent role in the alternative cycles. It constitutes the basis for analyzing seemingly nonsense words in *mantras,* Sanskrit phrases that are repeated to help maintain mindfulness of a Buddha-figure. It is also used to understand "seed-syllables" — Sanskrit letters that are either initial syllables or code names for a Buddha-figure or one of the elements. Like a seed, they are a trace of what they signify and out of which what they signify appears. During the empowerment, and later in meditational practice, we repeatedly imagine them at specific points in our body, and we generate various figures and objects from them. When we keep in mind the correlation between the five vowel families and the five elements, these otherwise bewildering visualizations start to make sense.

WARTIME AND PEACETIME TECHNOLOGY

The next section of the first chapter of the *Kalachakra Tantra* presents the technology for building weapons such as catapults and flamethrowers. Some people find it strange that a Buddhist text discusses how to wage an actual war, not just a symbolic one against our own delusions. Buddhism, after all, teaches non-violence. In explaining the meaning of true non-violence, His Holiness the Dalai Lama gives the following example.

Once there were two meditators sitting by the side of a rushing torrent, when a crazed man arrived intending to swim across. Both meditators knew that the current was extremely treacherous and that the man would surely drown. They tried to dissuade him from crossing, but the man would not listen to reason. One of the meditators decided that nothing could be done and so resumed his absorbed concentration. The other got up and punched the man unconscious so that he would not kill himself in the river. Who committed the act of violence? It was the meditator who shunned the opportunity to save a life. Thus, if all other means fail to end a drastic situation, then out of the wish to prevent others' suffering, and without anger or hatred, we need not hesitate to use forceful means. In doing so, however, we need to be willing to accept the painful consequences of our actions, even if it means hellish suffering. This is the conduct of a bodhisattva.

When the battle is won, wartime technology is turned over to peacetime purposes. Therefore the first chapter continues with instructions for building merry-go-rounds and other amusements for the public to celebrate victory, decorative fountains to ease their minds, and irrigation schemes to help with their livelihood. Establishing a peaceful, pleasant environment provides conducive circumstances for friendly relations between people to grow. Maintaining a high level of weaponry, on the other hand, is more likely to provide the circumstances for distrust and fear, and for people to use them.

THE GOLDEN AGE OF KALACHAKRA AND THE AGE OF AQUARIUS

The chapter ends with a prediction of a new golden age during which the spiritual practice of Kalachakra will flourish. Using the Hindu names of the four eras of a world age, but defining their lengths differently, it prophesies that the present *kaliyuga*, or dark age, will end with the defeat of the barbaric forces in this future war. The new golden era that dawns will begin in 2424, a date which corresponds within a few years to the start of the astronomical age of Aquarius, although the Kalachakra literature does not call it by that name.

The date for this shift of ages derives from a phenomenon known as the precession of the equinox, which refers to the equinox moving backwards. There are two commonly used zodiac systems in astronomy and astrology. According to the fixed star system used in all Indian traditions, including Kalachakra, when the sun is located at the beginning of the constellation Aries, its position is zero degrees Aries. This does not occur on the same day each year. In the sidereal system used by the Greeks and in the West, this position is linked with the solar calendar. Thus regardless of the actual constellation in the sky where the sun is located, its position on the vernal equinox in the northern hemisphere — the first day of spring, when the day and night are of equal length — is called zero degrees Aries. This position moves slightly backwards in the sky each year. Now it is in the constellation Pisces, the one immediately preceding Aries. When it enters the constellation Aquarius, the new golden age by that name begins. When New Age advocates assert the imminent dawning of the age of Aquarius, they are using astrological terminology for the Christian millenarian view.

The external cycles of time continue past the dawn of this new golden age. The universe again will pass through four eras, ending in another kaliyuga. At that point, the teachings of the present Buddha will disappear from our continent world. The Kalachakra teachings will then come to the next of the twelve continent worlds and the cycles will repeat. Thus ends the first chapter of the *Kalachakra Tantra*. As we have seen, it offers considerable advice for world peace, making it extremely worthwhile to study even if we attend the empowerment as an observer and never involve ourselves with its meditational practice.

CHAPTER FOUR
Internal Kalachakra

The second chapter of the *Kalachakra Tantra* deals with the internal cycles of time. It discusses the animate beings who live in the environments that pass through external cycles. Without some basic knowledge of the topics in this chapter, it is difficult to follow or understand many of the procedures of the empowerment. Although the material is complicated, a rough understanding of it is the key for gaining access to the profound Kalachakra techniques for achieving enlightenment.

THE FOUR MANNERS OF REBIRTH

The chapter begins with a discussion of the grossest internal cycle, which is the recurrence of death, bardo and rebirth. In general, Buddhism asserts four manners of rebirth: from a womb, from an egg, from heat and moisture, and by transformation. Since the Kalachakra system emphasizes purification of the elements, it classifies rebirths according to the element from which they occur. The birth of birds from an egg is called birth from wind, since most birds fly. The birth of mammals from a womb is called birth from fire, since the womb is warm. The birth of insects from heat and moisture is called birth from water, since so many insects are found around ponds in the summer. The birth of trees from the transformation of a seed in the ground is called birth from earth. Lastly, the birth of miraculous beings by great transformation, without any gestation period, is called birth from space, since they appear out of thin air without any obstruction.

The commentaries take great pains to explain that trees are mentioned only to complete the analogy and their inclusion among the states of rebirth is not to be taken literally. Although plants are a form of biological life, they cannot act with intention, make choices and, because of confusion, build up karmic potentials from willful behavior. This is because they do not have a mind — defined in Buddhism as mere clarity and awareness, the cognitive basis for karmic action. Only animate beings, known as "sentient beings" in Buddhist translations, have a mind. Nevertheless, the inclusion of trees in this list indicates that, like animate beings, they are worthy of respect and protection. Peace entails treating kindly not only people and creatures, but also the forests.

For human beings, birth may also be from either a womb, an egg, heat and moisture, or by transformation. This is not as odd as it might appear at first sight. Ordinary birth is from a womb. Birth from an egg is from a joined sperm and egg, but in a container different from the bare womb itself. Test-tube babies undoubtedly fall in this category. Birth from heat and moisture, in other words not from a sperm and egg, may refer to birth by cloning techniques. In the case of birth by transformation, the body is fully formed at the moment life begins. Rebirth as an android in a computerized body seems the closest equivalent. Although the Kalachakra texts do not speak explicitly about these future forms of human life, when we fit the classical Buddhist categories and descriptions with modern scientific advances we gain intellectual and ethical frameworks for integrating such persons into society.

WHAT CONTINUES FROM ONE LIFETIME TO THE NEXT

According to other tantric systems such as Guhyasamaja, the ever-changing stream of continuity of subtlest mind and subtlest energy-wind flows from one life to the next, regardless of the manner of rebirth, and proceeds even into Buddhahood. To return to the analogy of the radio that plays forever, if the subtlest mind is like a radio being on, subtlest energy-wind is like the electricity that powers it. A radio being on and the electricity powering it always come together in one "package." There cannot be one without the other. Likewise, subtlest mind and energy-wind are forever inseparable. In fact, all levels of mind operate on the basis of some form of energy-wind, from which they are indivisible.

Karmic "seeds" or tendencies, as well as karmic potentials, come along with the stream of continuity of our subtlest mind and energy-wind. They are not an integral part of the package, however. Like karma itself, they are subtle forms that merely give a temporary shape to the flow of our subtlest energy-wind. When enlightenment is attained, they are removed, like static disappearing from a perfectly tuned radio.

Vows are also subtle forms that travel with and shape the mind-stream, fashioning our physical, verbal and mental behavior. Although lay and monastic vows for individual liberation (*pratimoksha* vows) last only one lifetime, bodhisattva and tantric vows remain with the stream of continuity from one life to the next, shaping the mind-stream all the way until enlightenment. Vows are like the frequency of a specific radio wave to which a receiver can be finely tuned. Finally, because everyone's stream of continuity is individual, each can be referred to conventionally with a name, such as "me." This conventional identity marking the individuality of each stream is also part of the package that passes from one lifetime to the next and into enlightenment.

The Kalachakra system accepts and expands upon the Guhyasamaja presentation of these points, but uses its own distinctive terminology, such as winds of karma. It explains that inseparable from the package of subtlest mind and energy-wind, passing with it from one lifetime to the next and into enlightenment, are subtlest speech and a subtlest creative drop. Subtlest speech is the natural vibration or resonance of this subtlest package. The subtlest drop is a trace of earth, water, fire and wind particles, in a dissociated, condensed form. The continuity of this drop is like the stream of electrons — a trace of atoms — which comprises the electricity that keeps a radio on.

SUBTLEST CREATIVE DROPS AND SPACE PARTICLES

Subtlest drops are analogous to space particles. During empty eons between manifest periods of a universe there are no physical atoms, nevertheless a space particle endures as a condensed trace of the dissociated elemental particles of that universe. Like the matter sucked into a black hole, these traces are temporarily free of the physical laws that ordinarily govern universes made of grosser particles and atoms.

Likewise, during the period of our death existence, before our next rebirth state manifests with its associated bardo, a subtlest creative drop abides as part of our stream of continuity. It too consists of traces of elemental particles which are also temporarily free of the laws of karma that ordinarily regulate bodies made of atoms.

When the space particle of a universe is eventually affected by winds of the collective karma of many beings — marking the end of its empty eon — it acts as a kernel giving rise to the physical matter of the next phase of the universe. Likewise, when the subtlest creative drop is eventually affected by the winds of personal karma — marking the end of its period of death — it gives rise to the physical matter of an individual's next rebirth state. In the case of rebirth as a human or animal, this occurs in conjunction with the gross elements of a joined sperm and egg. Like a physical key, but not made of atoms, the subtlest creative drop unlocks the potential of a fertilized egg to grow and develop.

On the subtlest level, the physical processes of a universe and the karmic processes of a rebirth are based on a continuing stream, respectively, of space atoms and subtlest drops in a more evolved form. In the case of a universe, this is as the space between particles and, in the case of a human rebirth, as the subtle creative drops of the energy-system, which we shall discuss shortly.

DEVOID FORMS

There are several types of phenomena that have a form but are not made of gross particles or atoms. One class of these, discussed only in the Kalachakra system, is "devoid forms." These are forms that are devoid of atoms. They are not mental fabrications like the appearances in visualizations, dreams or the bardo state. Rather, they are the natural reflections of the clear light mind, which occur under specific circumstances, whether or not any of the grosser levels of mind are operating. The texts describe them like images appearing in a magic mirror, but without any mirror.

There are basis, pathway and resultant devoid forms. The colored spot that we see after looking away from a bright light is an example of a basis-level devoid form. It is not made of atoms, does not appear just in the imagination, and is seen non-conceptually with eyes open or shut. On a pathway level, devoid forms occur during the complete stage yogas once the energy-winds have been brought into the central channel. As a consequence of previous visualization practice, the subtlest mind then gives rise, within that channel, to devoid form bodies of the Buddha-figure Kalachakra, which are used to attain enlightenment. As a result of this practice, on a resultant level the omniscient clear light mind gives rise to a body of infinite devoid forms as Kalachakra, which are used to benefit others.

Since the aim of Kalachakra practice is to arise in pathway and resultant forms that are not made of atoms, we need to purify ourselves of our instinctive habit of basing the appearances our mind gives rise to on the atoms and particles of our internal and external elements. This is the reason why the elements are a dominant theme in the Kalachakra system and why they play such a prominent role in the initiation procedure. Several sections in the empowerment purify the elements by cleansing the mind of its habit of basing all appearances on them. In this way, the initiation plants seeds for arising in the enlightening devoid forms of a Buddha.

HUMAN REBIRTH

Having presented the process of death, bardo and rebirth, the *Kalachakra Tantra* now focuses on rebirth from a womb as a human. It delineates ten stages from conception to death, with the first three occurring as a fetus. As with the Guhyasamaja explanation of conception, the "package" of the bardo-being enters the future father's mouth and passes through his organ into the future mother's womb to start a new rebirth. We visualize this process happening to us during the inner empowerments of the Kalachakra initiation procedure when we are born as the spiritual child of our tantric master. It does not follow from this, however, that we need to take this procedure as describing what biologically happens when we take rebirth from a womb. Just as the various Buddhist descriptions of the universe are for specific purposes, likewise the anuttarayoga depiction of conception is for the purpose of showing that the clear light mind is naturally blissful, in harmony with the minds of the parents experiencing the bliss of union. On another level, it is to indicate the close link between the bliss of orgasmic release and the root of uncontrollably recurring rebirth, samsara. For deciding delicate ethical issues concerning abortion and contraception, it is therefore more appropriate to use modern scientific criteria for determining the start of a life.

The Kalachakra texts describe the ten stages of a human life by analogy with the Hindu presentation of the ten avatars of Vishnu. This provides an internal parallel for events in Shambhala. As the final avatar,

Kalki is symbolic of death. Just as Manjushri-yashas united his people in the Kalachakra mandala, death gathers all the jumbled energy-winds of the subtle body in the heart and dissolves them so as to manifest clear light subtlest mind. Furthermore, just as the twenty-fifth Kalki will defeat the barbarians in a future apocalypse, ushering in a golden age, death temporarily puts an end to all disturbing levels of mind and heralds the beginning of a new rebirth with the possibility for greater spiritual progress.

THE SUBTLE BODY

After describing in detail the development of a fetus, the second chapter continues by presenting the anatomy of both the gross and subtle human body. The subtle body, although made of particles, is invisible to the ordinary human eye, even if assisted by a microscope. It consists of energy-channels containing nodes called *chakras*, energy-winds, subtle vibrations or "speech," and creative drops. Thus, it is analogous to a universe consisting of planetary orbits, centrifugal energy, planetary speed and orbiting planets. These subtle channels, winds, speech and drops play a large role in the Kalachakra system, including the initiation. Let us therefore look at them more closely.

Just as the gross body has the visible channels of the circulatory, digestive and nervous systems, likewise the subtle body has invisible channels through which energy-winds flow. Chinese medicine presents a similar phenomenon in the form of invisible meridians used in acupuncture. Researchers of modern allopathic medicine are also currently investigating the existence of invisible pathways within the body. This is because messages of the immune system to deploy white blood cells do not pass through the nervous system or any other visible channels of communication.

The Tibetan term for subtle energy-channels, *tsa*, also means roots. If the gross body is like a plant above the surface of the ground, the channels are the invisible roots that connect it to its deepest level and source — the subtlest mind, energy-wind, speech and creative drop. Complete stage practice leads beneath the visible surface of the gross body to the chakras of the central channel and gains access through them to this subtlest, most subterranean level.

On a gross level, the winds of the breath course through the gross channels of the respiratory system, sustaining life in general. Similarly, subtle energy-winds course through the subtle channels providing the energy for motion, digestion and the functioning of the senses.

Complete stage practice involves techniques that cause these winds to dissolve at the chakras of the central channel, somewhat like water going down a drain and disappearing beneath the ground. Since mind is inseparable from these winds, this dissolution process brings the awareness to the subtle, subterranean level which is clear light mind.

Gross speech is the sound of the vibration of the breath within the respiratory channels of the nose, throat and lungs. Subtle speech is a parallel phenomenon that occurs in the subtle energy-system. Modern medicine seems to confirm the existence of this subtle resonance when it uses equipment to measure phenomena such as brain waves. Complete stage methods generate subtle sounds within the central energy-channel, which help draw the energy-winds there and dissolve. During the initiation and generation stage practice, we build up causes to accomplish this process by visualizing seed-syllables within the chakras of our central channel.

Just as winds of karma cause visible creative drops of sperm, semen, ovum and vaginal secretion to pass through gross channels of the visible body, likewise a wide assortment of subtle creative drops passes through the invisible channels of the subtle body. Perhaps the closest equivalent in Western medical science is the flow of hormones. Complete stage practice brings the ability to move these subtle drops at will and to position them in such a way that they support the clear light mind's blissful awareness of voidness.

THE FOUR SUBTLE CREATIVE DROPS

In addition to the drops that move through the channels of the subtle energy-system, there are four subtle creative drops that remain stationary throughout our life. These are the body, speech, mind and deep awareness drops located, respectively, at the center of the mid-brow, throat, heart and navel chakras. These are more gross than the subtlest drop inseparable from clear light mind and, like the gross body and the rest of the subtle energy-system, do not continue into death or Buddhahood.

When we are awake, dreaming, in dreamless sleep or in peak moments of orgasmic bliss, energy-winds of karma associated with each of these experiences gather, respectively, in the vicinity of the body, speech, mind or deep awareness creative drops, but not within the central channel. Our mind then projects the appearances it perceives during these states onto the basis of external or internal particles or atoms. The process is like one of artistic creation. Mind dips the energy-winds, like a brush, into one of four subtle drops, and paints appearances on the canvas of the atoms of our external or internal elements.

The winds of karma that are drawn to these drops, like iron filings to a magnet, carry the karmic potentials that obscure our experience of these four occasions so that they are associated with confusion. Thus we experience appearances of solid existence on the basis of our awake drop, confused speech on the basis of our dream drop, a blank unknowing mind on the basis of our deep sleep drop, and the bliss of orgasmic release on the basis of our deep awareness drop. These build up more winds of karma to perpetuate our continuing rebirth in forms that experience problems and suffering.

The appearances that mind gives rise to during these four occasions are deceptive because they arise under the influence of the karma and confusion that are carried by the winds of karma. It is as if the artist mind is using a dirty brush to paint. Appearances, in this context, are not merely visual forms, but also sounds, smells, tastes, and physical or tactile sensations. The mind makes all these forms appear to be solidly existent, whereas in reality nothing exists in this fantasized and impossible manner. After all, material phenomena are made of atoms. The mind simply connects the dots and makes them appear to be concrete and solid.

Eliminating the winds of karma through generating our clear light mind as an unchanging blissful awareness of voidness also removes the obscuration that these energy-winds carry. As a result, appearances of solid existence, confused speech and so on no longer arise. This is how the four subtle drops are purified. They are cleansed of their association with confused states of mind — a process which begins with the Kalachakra initiation.

CORRELATION WITH DESCRIPTIONS OF SUBTLE BODY IN OTHER SYSTEMS

The discussion of the four subtle drops, which is exclusive to Kalachakra literature, helps to explain many of the obscure points in other systems. For example, it is a common practice to focus on the mid-brow to awake from dullness or sleepiness during meditation. Only by reading the *Kalachakra Tantra* does it become clear that this is because the mid-brow is the location of the body drop, which is associated with being awake. Similarly, because the speech drop, associated with dreams, is located at the throat, focusing on the throat before going to sleep harnesses the dream state for practicing dream yoga. Because the mind drop associated with the non-conceptual state of deep dreamless sleep is located at the heart, concentrating on the heart chakra in clear light practices manifests subtlest mind. And it is because the deep awareness drop associated with peak blissful moments is located at the navel that the practice of *tummo,* or the inner flame, uses the navel chakra to generate blissful deep awareness to be used for understanding voidness.

The description of the energy-channels and chakras in the Kalachakra system diverges slightly from that found in the other anuttarayoga tantras, as represented by Guhyasamaja. On one level, just as the abhidharma and Kalachakra depictions of the universe differ due to their separate purposes, the same is true with the presentations of the channels and chakras in the two tantra systems. The Kalachakra teachings structure everything in terms of parallels between the external and internal worlds so as to model meditations analogous to both. Just as there are six elements in the world, in anatomy there are six main chakras along the central channel — at the crown of the head, forehead, throat, heart, navel and pubic region. During the Kalachakra empowerment, visualizations of different syllables and colored discs at these spots purify both the chakras and their associated elements.

We can also understand the different presentations of the body's subtle energy system as particularly suited to specific types of practitioners. We do not have just one type of subtle system, like a blood type, which can be determined in consultation with a tantric meditational master. Rather, each of us possesses the entire range of energy systems, somewhat like quantum levels. Work with a meditation master helps ascertain which of these systems is most prominent and easiest for us to access in order to reach the subtlest level of our mind so as to gain with it the most effective understanding of voidness.

KALACHAKRA AND TIBETO-MONGOLIAN MEDICINE

The presentation of the channels and chakras in Tibetan medicine is slightly different from that of both the Kalachakra and Guhyasamaja systems. In his medical commentaries, Desi Sanggyay-gyatso, the seventeenth-century minister of the Fifth Dalai Lama, has pointed out that this discrepancy is helpful. Otherwise people might simply read a medical text on anatomy and think that they could practice advanced tantric meditations involving the subtle energy-system without the close supervision and guidance of a qualified master. Approaching such meditations in a do-it-yourself manner is actually quite dangerous.

Although most of the Tibeto-Mongolian medical system derives from other Indian Buddhist sources, it does borrow a number of anatomical terms from the Kalachakra system. The sections of the central channel above and below the navel chakra, for example, are called Rahu and Kalagni, while the major right and left channels that intertwine around this chakra are called the sun and the moon. Thus the meeting of these four channels at the navel chakra parallels the structure of solar and lunar eclipses, when these four heavenly bodies likewise conjoin. This symbolism of an eclipse also occurs during the practices of the alternative cycles of time, including the empowerment, when we generate ourselves as the Buddha-figure Kalachakra standing on moon, sun, Rahu and Kalagni discs that are stacked like cushions on top of each other. This visualization contributes to the ability, in the complete stage practice, to gather the energy-winds at the navel chakra so that they eclipse, enter the central channel and dissolve. On another level, the white, red, black and yellow discs of these heavenly bodies symbolize, respectively, the body, speech, mind and deep awareness subtle drops that are purified and used for achieving the enlightening body, speech, mind and blissful deep awareness of a Buddha. The yellow disc is on top of the stack to indicate that the devoid form which is the immediate cause for achieving an enlightening Kalachakra body is generated first at the navel chakra, the location of the deep awareness drop.

THE CORRELATION OF INTERNAL AND EXTERNAL CYCLES

The second chapter continues the discussion of the human body by presenting the daily cycles through which it passes, all of which are analogous to external cycles of the universe. The most important internal cycle is that of the breath, since there is an intimate connection between breath and the energy-winds. The names for both are in fact the same. On an external level, if the period of a day and night is divided into sixty Kalachakra hours — there is no rule that it can only be divided into twenty-four — then in a 360-day lunar year, there are 21,600 hours. Similarly, if our energies are balanced, we breathe 21,600 times during the course of a day and night. This works out to one breath about every four modern seconds, which is accurate when we time our own respiration. Just as the sun travels half the year through the northern sector of the sky and half through the southern one — known astronomically as the sun's northern and southern declinations — likewise we breathe half the time predominantly through the right nostril and the other half through the left. If we put our hand beneath our nose, we can verify that we breathe mainly through one nostril at any time. Except for a few breaths during the shift from one nostril to the other, the breath normally does not pass evenly through both. Furthermore, just as the sun travels through the twelve zodiac signs during a year, likewise the breath shifts from one nostril to the other twelve times during a day and night. All these parallels have counterparts in the alternative Kalachakra system of practice.

THE LIFE-SPIRIT CYCLE AND GOOD HEALTH

The second chapter also discusses a special type of subtle creative drop which acts like a magnet attracting our life-spirit energy (Skt. *bodhichitta*; Tib. *bla*). This energy helps to keep our mind balanced. Losing it results in dysfunctional states such as nervous breakdown or shell shock. The life-spirit drop is the point of strongest potency of this energy, and it circulates around the body in a thirty-day cycle correlated to the phases of the moon. At each full moon, it is located at the crown of the head. During the waning moon it passes down one side of the body and during the waxing moon back up the other.

This phenomenon has medical application. Tibeto-Mongolian doctors, when time and circumstances permit, consult this cycle to choose the optimum day for performing, for example, moxibustion heat treatment for an arthritic joint. When an operation is performed on a certain spot in the body on the date of the lunar month when the life-spirit energy is most potent there, the body recovers more quickly. Perhaps this fact is related to cycles in the immune system. If the phases of the moon exert an influence on the strength of the tides, it is not unreasonable that they also affect the strength of the body's subtle energies.

The life-spirit cycle also helps us to understand certain enigmatic Buddhist teachings, for instance that it is best not to engage in sex on the full moon. When the subtle life-spirit drop is at the crown of the head, the life-spirit energies gather there. This provides the most conducive circumstance for bringing these and other energy-winds into the central channel through that juncture. Since orgasm releases subtle creative drops, including this life-spirit one, experiencing orgasm that day wastes the best opportunity in the month for dissolving the energy-winds and accessing clear light mind. The fact that on full moon days the life-spirit energy is most potent at the crown of the head — the most crucial point in the subtle body — may also account for particularly sensitive people noticing that their energies are affected by the full moon.

The internal cycles of time affect our health in general. In his fourteenth-century commentary on the second chapter of the *Kalachakra Tantra*, the Third Karmapa has explained how our confusion about reality causes cycles of the poisonous attitudes of attachment, anger and stubborn foolishness periodically to arise. These unbalanced attitudes bring on disease by precipitating an imbalance in the body's three corresponding physiological systems, known respectively as the humors of wind, bile and phlegm. Because Kalachakra practice eliminates confusion and ignorance, which are the roots of mental problems as well as physical disease, as the emotions become more balanced through meditative practice, the body naturally follows suit. Just as the external Kalachakra teachings provide guidelines for achieving world peace, the correlation in internal Kalachakra between emotional and physical health is one of the best guidelines for inner peace.

ALCHEMY

The last major topic of the second chapter is alchemy, the transformation of base substances into something useful and beneficial. First the text presents the formulas for making incense, for the purposes of disinfecting, healing and offering. It then explains how to transmute base metals, not into gold, but into medicine. The principal topic is how to detoxify mercury to render it usable as the main ingredient in preparing "precious pills."

As part of the internal cycles of time, new diseases periodically spread. Many of those prophesied in the text are related to pollution, which we can identify now as coming from chemicals, radiation and so on. The descriptions of the diseases seem also to include cancer and AIDS. Purified mercury detoxifies the body of pollutants and helps revitalize all of its systems. Tibetan doctors have used precious pills made from the Kalachakra formulas to successfully treat victims of the Bhopal chemical spill in India and the Chernobyl radiation disaster in the former Soviet Union, and are having modest success in at least prolonging the lives of some cancer and AIDS patients.

Parallel to the alchemical process, the alternative cycles present anuttarayoga tantra methods for transmuting the energy-winds that underlie disturbing emotions, such as longing desire, so as to make them useful along the spiritual path. Harnessing the energies of these emotions allows for an easier dissolution of other energy-winds in the body which are especially difficult to bring into the central channel. In this and other ways, the transmuted energy of desire acts like a precious medicine that helps access clear light mind and use its blissful deep awareness for focusing on voidness. The generation and use of blissful awareness for understanding voidness are major themes that repeat throughout the Kalachakra empowerment and meditational practices. Some knowledge of the internal cycles of time helps us to understand the physiology involved.

CHAPTER FIVE
Alternative Kalachakra

QUALIFICATIONS OF A KALACHAKRA MASTER

The third through fifth chapters of the *Kalachakra Tantra* present the alternative cycles of time. The third chapter, which concerns the empowerment, begins with a discussion of the qualifications of a Kalachakra tantric master and the procedures to follow regarding such a teacher before receiving initiation. It is extremely important to examine a tantric master with critical scrutiny before committing ourselves to be a disciple. Success in achieving the goal of enlightenment and the full ability to benefit others depends on the purity and honesty of our relation with our teacher. Only after establishing a close bond and gaining total confidence is it appropriate to request from a master Kalachakra empowerment. As most people do not have the fortune or opportunity to establish a close personal relationship with the great masters who currently confer Kalachakra initiation, the only alternative is to check such teachers from whatever contact is possible or to consider trustworthy firsthand accounts. Even if we cannot personally meet the master before the empowerment, it is far better to come for initiation on the stable foundation of confidence and trust gained through reason, rather than the shaky grounds of blind faith based on the person's name and fame. Since in most cases it is not possible to request empowerment beforehand in a private meeting, the request is made formally as part of the initial steps of the ceremony.

According to the third chapter of the *Kalachakra Tantra*, authentic tantric masters of this system have unbroken close bonds with their own teachers, the practices, their vows and the true nature of reality. Specifically, they keep the Kalachakra tantric vows purely and have meditated successfully on the Kalachakra generation and complete stages. They are free of attachment to anything, including their families, friends and even their bodies. Likewise they are unstained by greed, anger, foolish and stubborn ignorance, pride, jealousy or miserliness. With great patience, they work for the sake of their disciples with sincere interest in their welfare, and with no concern for personally gaining service, love, respect, fame or wealth. They are solely motivated by bodhichitta, the wish to become a Buddha to benefit others. Having achieved pathway minds that lead to enlightenment, they are able to guide others in also gaining these minds and thus free them from fears. Having attained unchanging blissful awareness focused on voidness, they remain completely chaste, never losing their blissful state of mind through orgasm's release.

Furthermore, Kalachakra tantric masters are stable, emotionally tamed, full of common-sense intelligence, patient, honest, unpretentious, brimming with loving concern for others, well versed in scripture and commentary, skilled in applying the tantric techniques, and totally familiar with all tantric ritual procedures. They have all the qualities and skills necessary to crush the four *maras*, or demonic interferences. According to the Kalachakra system, the four maras are our physical, verbal and mental obstacles or blocks, and the obstacles caused by belief in incorrect views of reality. The textual example of the latter is believing it is unnecessary to do anything constructive in life because all happiness comes as a gift of the gods.

If there are three qualified tantric masters available — a full monk, a novice and a householder — and, all else being equal, we need to choose from among them, the text says to rely on a fully ordained master. Devotion to a lay teacher in preference to a perfectly qualified monk undermines Buddha's teachings. This is because people seeing such a monk being bypassed gain the impression that the monastic community, representing the Sangha Jewel of Refuge — one of the Three Precious Gems that provide safe direction in life — is unnecessary. This is important to bear in mind in light of the tendency in the West to minimize the role and importance of monks and nuns in Buddhism and place the emphasis on laypersons.

IMPROPER TEACHERS

The third chapter also explains how to recognize an improper Kalachakra master. Such teachers are proud, filled with prejudice and hatred, have broken their close bonds with their teachers, vows and the practices, show disrespect for holy objects, and have studied little of the vast Kalachakra practices. They are only interested in deceiving their disciples, their minds have fallen from unchanging blissful awareness — if they had ever achieved it — and they teach without proper empowerment or meditational experience. They are attached to desirable objects of the senses, are not conscientious, use harsh language, and desire only the ephemeral bliss of sexual orgasm. The *Kalachakra Tantra* warns to avoid such teachers like a burning hell. Even if we request and go through the ritual procedures of tantric initiation with such so-called "gurus," we do not actually receive empowerment. This is because their shortcomings disqualify them from being capable of conferring it.

If we have already committed ourselves to such improper teachers, who lack compassion, are filled with anger, attached to sensory pleasures, arrogant and always praise themselves, the text advises to dissociate from them. Kaydrub Norzang-gyatso, the fifteenth-century tutor of the Second Dalai Lama, was careful to explain that this does not mean to disparage them and be disrespectful. Rather, we have nothing further to do with them. Since it is difficult to find a teacher with full qualifications, the only alternative is to rely on someone who at least has a majority of good qualities, most importantly someone who keeps the vows purely.

QUALIFICATIONS FOR RECEIVING EMPOWERMENT

The third chapter next explains the qualifications of disciples for receiving Kalachakra empowerment. We need to examine ourselves honestly to see if we meet the standard. According to the *Abbreviated Kalachakra Tantra*, proper disciples for full empowerment have deep interest in unchanging blissful awareness of voidness and devoid forms, and delight in restraining from destructive behavior and in strictly maintaining the tantric vows. They have given up distracting themselves with trivial endeavors, have no regard for wealth or possessions, have undying faith in the Triple Gem, and have no interest in worldly attainments from tantric practice, only enlightenment. Furthermore, they fully respect the tantric procedures, do not consider mere visualization or ritual practice to be sufficient, are able to keep the guideline instructions for the complete stage confidential until they have gained realization of them, and do not closely associate with those who might deter them from their practice or goal.

The *Stainless Light* commentary adds that proper disciples for any level of Kalachakra empowerment have begun their serious spiritual training by receiving and keeping lay vows to avoid killing, stealing, lying, indulging in inappropriate sexual behavior and taking intoxicants. For those who have not had the opportunity to take these vows beforehand, they are included among the twenty-five modes of tamed behavior initiates pledge to uphold as part of the empowerment. We shall examine the meaning and implications of this pledge when we discuss these types of tamed behavior in chapter eight.

Furthermore, with a firm foundation of ethical self-discipline, proper disciples have developed a mahayana mind imbued with love, compassion, exceptional resolve and bodhichitta, and have come to hold a madhyamaka view of reality by having studied, in stages, the less sophisticated Buddhist tenet systems. Gradually working up to a madhyamaka view ensures a deeper understanding which is more firmly based.

Since every step of the Kalachakra empowerment and practice is founded on bodhichitta and an understanding of voidness, at least some familiarity with them is necessary beforehand. The text does not state specifically what level of competence this need be. However, following basic Buddhist guidelines is always a safe criterion. An engaged practitioner is more interested in future lives than in this one, more interested in liberation from samsara than in gaining a better future rebirth, more interested in helping others than in satisfying selfish desires, and more interested in seeing the reality of things than in unquestioningly accepting appearances. Even if we have not studied voidness or meditated on it deeply, we need at least to take sincere interest in it and intend to pursue it more seriously as soon as possible.

Finally, the *Stainless Light* states that before empowerment disciples need to have fervent regard and respect for the methods of anuttarayoga tantra, and specifically those of Kalachakra. To gain this admiration and interest, some level of study and intellectual understanding is indispensable.

DECIDING WHETHER TO ATTEND THE EMPOWERMENT

Many people would prefer to ask an authority if they are prepared or suited for Kalachakra practice. It is very rare, however, to have such an opportunity, and few have a close enough personal relationship with a spiritual master for consultation to be meaningful. We basically need to decide for ourselves if we are ready for tantra, and specifically for Kalachakra.

Many different motivations bring people to the Kalachakra initiation. Some persons are already deeply involved with another anuttarayoga tantra system and want to study Kalachakra to gain a clearer understanding of their other tantric practices. Some are practitioners who are not certain which Buddha-figure best suits them and wish to widen their options by including Kalachakra. Many do not feel ready for anuttarayoga practice, but attend simply to observe and to establish a karmic connection with the practice to pursue it in the future. However, if we are serious about practicing Kalachakra itself, how do we know it is right for us?

The main factor to consider in choosing an anuttarayoga system is the style of its complete stage practice. We need to identify our dominant subtle energy-system and determine which complete stage methods most effectively and suitably use that system to bring us access to our clear light mind. We can only ascertain this from meditational experience gained through study and experimentation with several systems, under the close supervision of a qualified tantric master. Having established the most appropriate complete stage style, then when we are prepared to devote full time to its practice, we focus intensely on the corresponding generation stage that ripens into success for that effort. The usual custom before reaching this point of certitude is to engage in a certain amount of generation stage practice of several anuttarayoga systems — as many and broad a spectrum as fit our capacity — so as to establish the karmic connections and familiarity necessary to make a final choice of systems.

The question still remains how to decide whether to include Kalachakra within the sphere of our anuttarayoga practice. We gauge our affinity by simply examining our natural interests. Although the texts do not elaborate this point, those who are intrigued with astronomy, astrology, nuclear physics, mathematics, technology, history or conflict resolution, and who feel drawn toward the external and internal Kalachakra discussions of these points, most likely have some connection with Kalachakra. We can conclude the same if our life is very complex, we need to juggle many things each day, and we are naturally attracted to the positive self-image Kalachakra represents — the ability to handle all situations no matter what the time or how many there might be.

Holding a Kalachakra self-image at moments of need and reciting appropriate mantras to maintain mindfulness of it are of great benefit even for people who never engage in a more serious level of Kalachakra meditation. In modern societies, many people lead fragmented lives, feeling alienated from vital components such as their body, feelings, creativity or parents. It is difficult to balance and integrate everything. It is as if we lead many lives at once — a public life and a private one, an office life, a family life, and social, professional, intellectual, spiritual, sports, club, holiday, leisure and political lives as well. The situation becomes even more complicated when there are divorces and remarriages. Kalachakra represents the ability to be a whole person, to fit all these elements together harmoniously.

The Kalachakra self-image derives from visualizing and identifying with all 722 figures of a complex mandala at the same time. When we are overwhelmed with work at the office and our supervisor places yet another project on our desk, if we remember the Kalachakra self-image, we do not become upset. It is like adding another group of figures in one of the corners of our huge mandala world. We can handle it easily. Thus even if we do not choose Kalachakra as our main practice, or even consider it as an option for future focus, we may elect to receive the Kalachakra empowerment in order to develop and work with its conventional self-image.

THE MANDALA USED FOR CONFERRING EMPOWERMENT

Having discussed the qualifications of the tantric master and disciples for the empowerment, the *Kalachakra Tantra* next discusses the type of mandala from which the ceremony is given. During the empowerment, we are led into the three-dimensional mandala world of Kalachakra and actually conferred empowerment in this mandala. This mandala is made of transparent clear light and is an emanation of the enlightening mind of the tantric master as the Buddha-figure. Those without an extremely advanced realization cannot actually see that mandala. During the initiation, most people merely imagine it to be present. There needs to be a basis, however, for this visualization to be a valid cognition.

We can understand the necessity for this from the example of mental labeling. Consider the example of building a new house. A house cannot be built without a mental scheme or an architect's blueprint or model, but the house itself is not any of these representations. No one is going to live in the tiny model. We can only speak of the specific house on the basis, for example, of a drawing. If there is no scheme, we can only speak of a new house in general, not the specific one we intend to build. The house is not the word "house," but is what that word refers to on the basis of the drawing. In Buddhist terminology, the drawing or model is the basis for mentally labeling the house. We cannot deal with a house except in terms of a basis for labeling one. When the house is actually built, the basis for labeling it is its rooms.

To deal with the Kalachakra mandala during initiation, there must also be a basis for labeling it. According to Naropa's eleventh-century Indian commentary to the third chapter, for Kalachakra empowerment that basis must be a mandala made of colored powders. If there are no resources available for constructing such a mandala, and the disciples are extremely well qualified, tantric masters may confer empowerment on the basis of a mandala emanated from their clear light mind and maintained by the power of their stable concentration. This is the only exception aside from the special occasion when King Manjushri-yashas used the full-scale three-dimensional replica of the mandala built in the royal park of Shambhala to unite his people. Nowadays, however, when resources are not available, many masters confer the empowerment on the basis of a mandala drawn on cloth.

THE THREE LEVELS OF EMPOWERMENT

The Kalachakra initiation consists of many different individual empowerments and, depending on how many are included, a Kalachakra master can confer the overall initiation on three levels of extensiveness. All levels of the initiation contain a set of seven empowerments known as the "seven of entering like a child." Each of these seven is analogous to a stage in human development from birth to youth. Beyond the seven of entering like a child, there are higher and highest sets of vase, secret, wisdom and fourth, or word empowerments, as well as the great vajra master empowerment.

On the first level of extensiveness, the master only imparts the seven of entering like a child. Receiving them empowers us to engage in the generation stage practices. On the second level, eleven empowerments are conferred: the seven of entering like a child, the higher vase, secret and wisdom empowerments, and then both the higher and highest fourth empowerments, which are counted as one. This second level empowers us to meditate on both the generation and complete stages of Kalachakra practice. The fullest level of initiation has the seven empowerments of entering like a child, the four higher and four highest empowerments, and the great vajra master initiation. It empowers those who gain actual attainments through generation and complete stage practice to confer Kalachakra initiation to others. Since most of us do not have a pressing need at the moment for this final empowerment, we need not pout if the level of initiation we receive is not the fullest. We are not missing anything we need right now, even if we receive only the first-level Kalachakra empowerment.

In addition to these three levels of empowerment, there is also a Kalachakra subsequent permission ceremony. Westerners often do not differentiate between an empowerment and a subsequent permission — a *wang* and a *jenang* — and use the term "initiation" for both. This causes confusion. Tsenzhab Serkong Rinpochey often used the analogy that receiving an empowerment is like being given a sword, while receiving subsequent permission is like having that sword sharpened for more effective use. The Kalachakra subsequent permission adds further inspiration for using body, speech and mind in an enlightening manner along the spiritual path to benefit others. The subsequent permission ceremony may be added after any of the three levels of empowerment. Even if it is not included, the initiation is still complete. We have the sword. Once we gain some experience using it, we can have it sharpened.

The third chapter next presents the preparations a master needs to make before conferring empowerment, including how to consecrate the ground and establish a protected space to ward off interference during the ceremony. Finally, it details the procedures for each empowerment. We shall look at some of these points in subsequent chapters.

APPROACHING THE COMPLEXITY OF KALACHAKRA PRACTICE

The fourth and fifth chapters present the generation and complete stage practices and describe the attainment of enlightenment through this path. These can be studied after receiving empowerment. Many people worry, however, that since the Kalachakra mandala contains 722 figures that are supposed to be visualized all at the same time in full detail, Kalachakra practice is too difficult. There is no need, however, to feel intimidated. Although Kalachakra practice is not simple, we do not begin meditation on its generation stage by attempting to visualize the entire thing. We usually start with a simplified sadhana scheme involving either one or two figures, with just one face and two arms. As our ability increases, we expand our visualization in specific increments until we are able to imagine the full mandala. Although study and practice of another anuttarayoga tantra, particularly Guhyasamaja, may be helpful before attempting Kalachakra, it is not a prerequisite.

Kalachakra does not hold the record for having the most figures in its mandala, but there are certainly enough. The mandala contains figures representing the 360 days of the year, the signs of the zodiac, the major constellations and planets, as well as most of the components of the human body, such as the bones, sensory apparatus, and the winds, channels and chakras of the subtle energy-system. Since our body and mind, and life itself, are so complex, with such numerous components, it takes an intricate scheme to symbolize, integrate and work with them all. Thus, all phases of Kalachakra practice, including the empowerment, are more elaborate than in most other tantras. The theory behind this is that because the mandala symbolizes the basis to be purified, a more extensive mandala results in a more thorough purification. This does not mean, however, that after receiving the Kalachakra initiation we must embark on a detailed study of Tibeto-Mongolian astrology and medicine to gain the widest possible knowledge of the basis to be purified. Acquaintance with their general principles is quite sufficient. Our main focus is on the alternative Kalachakra system.

Kalachakra complete stage practice brings the attainment of unique immediately preceding causes for an enlightening body and mind of a Buddha — namely, a devoid form and an unchanging blissful awareness of voidness. The enlightenment achieved by means of them, however, is the same as that attained through any other Buddhist technique. When some classical Tibetan texts state that Kalachakra is the pinnacle of all tantras, their praise is due to the extensiveness and clarity of the Kalachakra material, not the resultant stage achieved through its practice.

CHAPTER SIX

Refuge Commitments and Bodhisattva Vows

STUDYING THE COMMITMENTS AND VOWS

Most people who consider taking the Kalachakra initiation as active participants, rather than observers, are greatly concerned about the vows. They want to know what their commitments are so they can realistically assess their ability to keep them. Such honesty and conscientiousness are extremely praiseworthy. Traditionally, however, aspiring practitioners study only lay and bodhisattva vows before taking them, but do not learn the details of the monastic or tantric ones until they have actually promised to keep them. The idea is that renunciation is so strong to enter monastic life, and bodhichitta so compelling to engage in tantric practice, that genuine seekers are willing to do anything. Nowadays, however, people are particularly critical and cautious. Misinformation and confusion about tantra abound. For these reasons, the great Buddhist masters have sanctioned publication of clear explanations of all sets of vows for study and scrutiny by those sincerely interested in taking them.

ACTIONS TO ADOPT AFTER FORMALLY TAKING REFUGE

As refuge is the basis for all Buddhist vows, the first commitment we make as a participant at a Kalachakra initiation is to take refuge. Taking refuge means formally putting the safe and positive direction in our life indicated by the Triple Gem — the Buddhas, Dharma and Sangha — and pledging to maintain this steady direction unwaveringly, until it brings us enlightenment. Taking formal refuge at an empowerment is equivalent to doing so in a separate ceremony with a teacher. Cutting a lock of hair and receiving a Dharma name are not essential components of the procedure and are dispensed with when taking refuge at an initiation, even if it is for the first time.

When we formally orient our life with the safe and positive direction of refuge, we commit ourselves to three sets of actions helpful for maintaining this direction. The first set consists of eight actions that relate to general behavior. The eight are: parallel to taking safe direction from the Buddhas, (1) committing ourselves wholeheartedly to a spiritual teacher. If we do not have access to the master conferring the empowerment and have not yet found a personal teacher to direct our practice, this commitment is to find one.

Taking formal refuge with a teacher in a separate ceremony that is not part of a tantric initiation does not imply necessarily committing ourselves to following this teacher as our personal spiritual guide. It is important, of course, always to maintain respect and gratitude toward this person as the one who opened the door to our safe direction in life. Our refuge, however, is in the Triple Gem — represented by a Buddha statue or painting during the ceremony — and not in the specific person who conducts the ritual. Only within the context of a tantric initiation does the teacher embody the Three Jewels of Refuge and does taking safe direction create the formal bond of spiritual master and disciple. Furthermore, regardless of context, our safe direction is that of the Triple Gem in general, not that of a specific lineage or tradition of Buddhism. If the teacher conducting a refuge ceremony or initiation is of a particular lineage, receiving safe direction or empowerment from him or her does not necessarily render us a follower of the same lineage.

To maintain a Dharma direction in life, (2) studying the Buddhist teachings and (3) applying them to overcome our disturbing emotions and attitudes. Academic study is not enough. To take direction from the Sangha community of highly realized practitioners, (4) following their example. To do so does not mean necessarily becoming a monastic, but rather making sincere efforts to realize straightforwardly and non-conceptually the four true facts of life — the "four noble truths."

These are that life is difficult; that our difficulties come from a cause, namely confusion about reality; that we can end our problems; and that to do so we need the understanding of voidness as a pathway mind.

(5) Making working on ourselves the primary task in our life. This means rather than constantly complaining or criticizing others, devoting our time and energies to overcoming our shortcomings and realizing our talents and potentials. (6) Adopting the ethical standards the Buddhas have set. This ethic is based on clearly discriminating between what is helpful and what is harmful to a positive direction in life. Therefore, following the Buddhist ethic means to refrain from certain modes of conduct because they are destructive and hamper our ability to benefit ourselves or others, and to embrace other modes because they are constructive and help us to grow. (7) Trying to be as sympathetic and compassionate to others as possible. Even if our spiritual goal is limited to gaining liberation from our personal problems, this is never at the expense of others. Finally, to maintain our connection with the Triple Gem, (8) making special offerings of fruit, flowers and so forth on Buddhist holy days, such as the anniversary of Buddha's enlightenment. Observing religious holidays with traditional ritual helps us feel part of a larger community.

ACTIONS TO AVOID AND WAYS TO SHOW RESPECT

The second set of refuge commitments is to avoid certain actions and to maintain others, in connection with each of the Three Precious Gems. The actions avoided lead to a contrary direction in life, while those adopted foster mindfulness of the goal. The three actions to shun are: in spite of taking safe direction from the Buddhas, (1) taking paramount direction from elsewhere. The most important thing in life is no longer accumulating as many material objects and entertaining experiences as possible, but as many good qualities as we can — such as love, patience, concentration and wisdom — in order to be of more benefit to others. This is not a vow of poverty and abstinence, but rather an affirmation of having a deeper direction in life.

More specifically, this commitment means not taking ultimate refuge in gods or spirits. Buddhism, particularly in its Tibetan form, often contains ritual ceremonies, or *pujas*, directed toward various Buddha-figures or fierce protectors in order to help dispel obstacles and accomplish constructive purposes. Performing these ceremonies provides conducive circumstances for negative potentials to ripen in trivial rather than major obstacles, and positive potentials to ripen sooner rather than later. If we have built up overwhelmingly negative potentials, however, these ceremonies are ineffective in averting difficulties. Therefore, propitiating gods, spirits, protectors or even Buddhas is never a substitute for attending to our karma — avoiding destructive conduct and acting in a constructive manner. Buddhism is not a spiritual path of protector-worship, or even Buddha-worship. The safe direction of the Buddhist path is working to become a Buddha ourselves.

In spite of taking safe direction from the Dharma, (2) causing harm or mischief to humans or animals. One of the main guidelines Buddha taught is to help others as much as possible, and if we cannot be of help, at least not to cause any harm. And, in spite of taking direction from the Sangha, (3) associating closely with negative people. Shunning such contact helps us avoid being easily swayed from our positive goals when we are still weak in our direction in life. It does not mean having to live in a Buddhist community, but rather exercising care about the company we keep and taking whatever measures are appropriate and necessary to avoid detrimental influences.

The three actions to adopt as a sign of respect are honoring (4) all statues, paintings and other artistic depictions of Buddhas, (5) all books, especially concerning the Dharma, and (6) all persons with Buddhist monastic vows, and even their robes. Traditionally, signs of disrespect are stepping on or over such objects, sitting or standing on them, and placing them directly on the floor or ground without at least providing a piece of cloth beneath them. Although these objects are not the actual sources of safe direction, they represent and help keep us mindful of enlightened beings, their supreme attainments and the highly realized practitioners well-advanced toward that goal.

GENERAL REFUGE COMMITMENTS
The third set of commitments from refuge is to engage in six trainings that relate to the Three Precious Gems as a whole. The six are: (1) reaffirming our safe direction by continually reminding ourselves of the qualities of the Three Jewels of Refuge, and the difference between them and other possible directions in life. (2) In gratitude for their kindness and spiritual sustenance, offering the first portion of our hot drinks and meals each day to the Triple Gem. This is usually done in the imagination, although we may also place a small portion of our first hot drink of the day before a Buddha statue or painting, and then

later drink it ourselves. It is not necessary, when making offerings of food or drink, to recite a verse in a foreign tongue we do not know, unless we find its mystery inspiring. Simply thinking, "Please, Buddhas, enjoy this," is sufficient. If the people with whom we are eating are not Buddhists, it is best to make this offering in a discreet manner so that no one knows what we are doing. Making a show of our practice only invites others' discomfort or ridicule.

(3) Mindful of the compassion of the Triple Gem, indirectly encouraging others to go in their direction. The intent of this commitment is not that we become missionaries and try to convert anyone. However, people receptive to us who are lost in life, with either no direction or a negative one, often find it helpful if we explain to them the importance and benefit we ourselves derive from having a safe and positive direction. Whether or not others become Buddhists is not the point. Our own example may encourage them to do something constructive with their lives by working on themselves to grow and improve.

(4) Remembering the benefits of having a safe direction, formally reaffirming it three times each day and three times each night — usually in the morning shortly after waking up and in the evening just before going to sleep. This affirmation is normally made by repeating, "I take safe direction from the teachers, the Buddhas, the Dharma and the Sangha." The spiritual teachers do not constitute a fourth precious gem, but provide access to the three. In the context of tantra, the spiritual masters embody them all.

(5) Whatever happens, relying on our safe direction. In times of crisis, safe direction is the best refuge because it deals with adversity by seeking to eliminate its cause. Friends may give us sympathy, but unless they are enlightened beings, they inevitably let us down. They have problems of their own and are limited in what they can do. Always working to overcome shortcomings and difficulties in a sober and realistic manner, however, never fails in our hour of need. This leads to the final commitment, (6) never giving up this direction in life, no matter what happens.

TAKING REFUGE AND FOLLOWING OTHER RELIGIONS OR SPIRITUAL PATHS

Some people ask if taking refuge vows means converting to Buddhism and leaving forever their native religion. This is not the case, unless we wish to do so. There is no term in Tibetan literally equivalent to a "Buddhist." The word used for a practitioner means "someone who lives within," namely within the boundaries of taking a safe and positive direction in life. To live that type of life does not require wearing a red protection string around our neck and never setting foot inside a church, synagogue, Hindu temple or Confucian shrine. Rather, it means working on ourselves to overcome our shortcomings and realize our potentials — in other words, to actualize the Dharma — as the Buddhas have done and highly realized practitioners, the Sangha, are doing. We put our primary efforts in this direction. As many Buddhist masters have said, including my own late teacher, Tsenzhab Serkong Rinpochey, if we look at the teachings of charity and love in other religions such as Christianity, we must conclude that following them is not counter to the direction taught in Buddhism. The humanitarian message in all religions is the same.

Our safe and positive direction of refuge is primarily to refrain from the ten most destructive actions — taking the life of any living creature, taking what is not given, indulging in inappropriate sexual behavior, lying, speaking divisively, using harsh and cruel language, chattering meaninglessly, and thinking in either a covetous, malicious or distorted, antagonistic manner. Taking the Buddhist direction in life entails turning from only those teachings in other religious, philosophical or political systems that encourage action, speech or thought involving these destructive actions, and which is harmful to ourselves and others. Furthermore, although there is no prohibition against going to church, maintaining a steady direction means not to focus all our energies on that aspect of our life and neglect our Buddhist study and practice.

Some people wonder if taking refuge as part of a tantric ceremony will require them to stop practicing zen or systems of physical training such as hatha yoga or martial arts. The answer is no, because these are also methods to realize our positive potentials and do not compromise our safe direction in life. All great masters advise, however, not to mix and adulterate meditational practices. If we wish to have soup and a cup of coffee for lunch, we do not pour the coffee into the soup and drink both together. Engaging in several different trainings each day is fine. However, it is best to do them in separate sessions, carrying out each practice by honoring its individual customs. Just as it would be preposterous to offer three prostrations to the altar on entering a church, likewise it is inappropriate to recite mantras during a zen or vipassana meditation session.

ACTIONS FOR NEVER LOSING BODHICHITTA RESOLVE

The first set of vows we take as a participant at a Kalachakra initiation, and at empowerments into any class of tantra, is the bodhisattva vows. Bodhisattvas are those with bodhichitta — a heart totally dedicated to others and to achieving enlightenment in order to benefit them fully. There are two levels of bodhichitta: aspiring and involved. Aspiring bodhichitta is the strong wish to overcome our shortcomings and realize our potentials to benefit everyone. Involved bodhichitta means engaging in the practices that bring about this goal and taking bodhisattva vows to restrain from actions detrimental to it. The difference between the two levels is similar to that between wishing to become a doctor and actually entering medical school. Aspiring bodhichitta has the stages of merely wishing to become a Buddha for the benefit of others and pledging never to abandon this aim until it is achieved. Before taking bodhisattva vows at a Kalachakra empowerment, we formally generate these two stages of aspiration.

The pledge never to forsake the bodhisattva aim involves a promise to train in five types of actions that help us never to lose our resolve. (1) Each day and night recalling the advantages of the bodhichitta motivation. Just as we readily overcome our tiredness and tap our energies when we need to attend to our children, we easily surmount all difficulties and use all our potentials when our primary motivation in life is bodhichitta. (2) Reaffirming and strengthening this motivation by rededicating our heart to enlightenment and others three times each day and three times each night. (3) Striving to build up bountiful stores of positive potential and deep awareness, usually translated as "collections of merit and insight." In other words, helping others as effectively as we can, and doing so with as much deep awareness of reality as possible. (4) Never giving up trying to help anyone, or at least wishing to be able to do so, no matter how difficult he or she may be. (5) Ridding ourselves of four murky types of behavior and adopting four glowing ones instead.

The four pairs of behavior in this fifth pledge are as follows: (1) Stopping ever deceiving our spiritual teachers, parents and the Triple Gem. Instead, always being honest with them, especially about our motivation and efforts to help others. (2) Stopping ever faulting or being contemptuous of bodhisattvas. Instead, since only Buddhas can be certain who actually are bodhisattvas, regarding everyone in a pure way as our teacher. Even if people act in a crude and distasteful manner, they teach us not to behave in this way. (3) Stopping ever causing others to regret anything positive they have done. If someone makes numerous mistakes when typing a letter for us and we yell with outrage, the person may never offer to help again. Instead, encouraging others to be constructive and, if receptive, to work on overcoming their shortcomings and realizing their potentials to be of more benefit to everyone. Lastly, (4) stopping ever being hypocritical or pretentious in our dealings with others, in other words hiding our faults and pretending to have qualities we lack. Instead, taking responsibility to help others, always being honest and frank about our limitations and abilities. It is very cruel to promise more than we can deliver, raising others' false hopes.

ROOT BODHISATTVA VOWS

Taking bodhisattva vows entails promising to restrain from two sets of negative acts — eighteen actions that, if committed, constitute a root downfall; and forty-six types of faulty behavior. A root downfall means a loss of the entire set of bodhisattva vows. It is a "downfall" in the sense that it leads to a decline in spiritual development and hinders the growth of positive qualities. The word "root" signifies it is a root to be eliminated. For ease of expression, these two sets are sometimes called "root and secondary bodhisattva vows." They offer excellent guidelines for the types of behavior to avoid if we wish to benefit others in as pure and full a way as possible.

The promise to keep bodhisattva vows applies not only to this life, but to each subsequent lifetime until enlightenment. Thus these vows continue on our mind-stream into future lives. If we have taken the vows in a previous lifetime, we do not lose them by committing an infraction now unless we have taken them freshly during our current life. Retaking the vows for the first time in this life strengthens the momentum of our efforts toward enlightenment that has been growing ever since our first taking of them. Therefore, mahayana masters emphasize the importance of dying with the bodhisattva vows intact and strong. Their abiding presence on our mind-stream continues building up positive potential in future lives even before we revitalize them by taking them again.

Following the Gelug founder Tsongkapa's fifteenth-century commentary on the bodhisattva vows, let us look first at the eighteen negative actions that constitute a root downfall. Each has several stipulations we need to know.

(1) Praising ourselves and/or belittling others. This downfall refers to speaking such words to someone in an inferior position. The motivation must contain either desire for profit, praise, love, respect and so on from the person addressed, or jealousy of the person belittled. It makes no difference whether what we say is true or false. Professionals who advertize that they are Buddhists need to take care about committing this downfall.

(2) Not sharing Dharma teachings or wealth. Here the motivation must be specifically attachment and miserliness. This negative action includes not only being possessive of our notes or tape recorder, but also being stingy with our time and refusing to help if needed.

(3) Not listening to others' apologies or striking others. The motivation for either of these must be anger. The first refers to an actual occasion when yelling at or beating someone and either that person pleads for forgiveness or someone else begs us to stop and we refuse. The latter is simply hitting someone. Sometimes, it may be necessary to give rambunctious children or pets a smack to stop them from running into the road if they will not listen, but it is never appropriate or helpful to discipline out of anger.

(4) Discarding the mahayana teachings and propounding made-up ones. This means to reject the correct teachings about some topic concerning bodhisattvas, such as their ethical behavior, and to make up in their stead a plausible yet misleading instruction on the same subject, claim it to be authentic and then teach it to others in order to gain their following. An example of this downfall is when teachers who are eager not to scare away prospective students condone liberal moral behavior and explain that any type of action is acceptable so long as it does not harm others. We need not be a teacher to commit this downfall. We can commit it even in casual conversation with others.

(5) Taking offerings intended for the Triple Gem. This downfall is to steal or embezzle, either personally or through deputing someone else, anything offered or belonging to the Buddhas, Dharma or Sangha, and then to consider it as ours. The Sangha, in this context, refers to any group of four or more monastics. Examples include embezzling funds donated for building a Buddhist monument, for printing Dharma books or for feeding a group of monks or nuns.

(6) Forsaking the holy Dharma. Here the downfall is to repudiate or, by voicing our opinion, cause others to repudiate that the scriptural teachings of either the shravaka, pratyekabuddha or mahayana vehicles are the Buddha's words. Shravakas are those who listen to a

Buddha's teachings while they are still extant, while pratyekabuddhas are self-evolving practitioners who live primarily during dark ages when the Dharma is no longer directly available. To make spiritual progress, they rely on intuitive understanding gained from study and practice conducted during previous lives. The teachings for both of them collectively constitute the hinayana, or "modest vehicle" for gaining personal liberation from samsara. The mahayana vehicle emphasizes methods for attaining full enlightenment. Denying that all or just certain scriptures of either vehicle derive from the Buddha is a root downfall.

Maintaining this vow does not mean forsaking a historical perspective. Buddha's teachings were transmitted orally for centuries before being committed to writing, and thus corruptions and forgeries undoubtedly occurred. The great masters who compiled the Tibetan Buddhist canon certainly rejected texts they considered unauthentic. However, instead of basing their decisions on prejudice, they used Dharmakirti's criterion for assessing the validity of any material — the ability of its practice to bring about the Buddhist goals of better rebirth, liberation or enlightenment. Stylistic differences among Buddhist scriptures, and even within a specific text, often indicate differences in time when various portions of the teachings were written down or translated into different languages. Therefore, studying the scriptures through methods of modern textual analysis can often be fruitful and does not conflict with this vow.

(7) Disrobing monastics or committing such acts as stealing their robes. This downfall refers specifically to doing something damaging to one, two or three Buddhist monks or nuns, regardless of their moral status or level of study or practice. Such actions need to be motivated by ill-will or malice, and include beating or verbally abusing them, confiscating their goods or expelling them from their monastery. Expelling monastics, however, is not a downfall if they have broken one of their four major vows: not to kill, especially another human being; not to steal, particularly something belonging to the monastic community; not to lie, specifically about spiritual attainments; and to maintain complete celibacy.

(8) Committing any of the five heinous crimes. These are killing our father, mother or an *arhat* (a liberated being), with bad intentions drawing blood from a Buddha, or causing a split in the monastic community.

(9) Holding a distorted, antagonistic outlook. This means to deny what is true and of value — such as the laws of behavioral cause and

effect, a safe and positive direction in life, rebirth and liberation from it — and to be antagonistic toward such ideas and those who hold them.

(10) Destroying places such as towns. This downfall includes intentionally demolishing, bombing or degrading the environment of a town, city, district or countryside area, and rendering it unfit, harmful or difficult for humans or animals to live in.

(11) Teaching voidness to those whose minds are untrained. The primary objects of this downfall are persons with the bodhichitta motivation who are not yet ready to understand voidness. Such persons would become confused or frightened by this teaching and consequently abandon the bodhisattva path for the path of personal liberation. This can happen as a result of thinking that if all phenomena are devoid of inherent, findable existence, then no one exists, so why bother working to benefit anyone else? This action also includes teaching voidness to anyone who would misunderstand it and therefore forsake the Dharma completely, for example by thinking that Buddhism teaches that nothing exists and is therefore sheer nonsense. Without extrasensory perception, it is difficult to know whether others' minds are sufficiently trained so that they will not misconstrue the teachings on the voidness of all phenomena. Therefore it is important to lead others to these teachings through explanations of graduated levels of complexity, and periodically to check their understanding.

(12) Turning others away from full enlightenment. The objects for this action are people who have already developed a bodhichitta motivation and are striving toward enlightenment. The downfall is to tell them they are incapable of acting all the time with generosity, patience and so on — to say that they cannot possibly become a Buddha and so it would be far better for them to strive merely for their own liberation. Unless they actually turn their aim away from enlightenment, however, this root downfall is incomplete.

(13) Turning others away from their pratimoksha vows. Pratimoksha, or individual liberation vows, include those for laypersons, novices and full monks and nuns. The objects here are persons who are keeping one of these sets of pratimoksha vows. The downfall is to tell them as a bodhisattva there is no use in keeping pratimoksha because for bodhisattvas all actions are pure. For this downfall to be complete, they must actually give up their vows.

(14) Belittling the shravaka vehicle. The sixth root downfall is to repudiate that the texts of the shravaka or pratyekabuddha vehicles are the authentic words of the Buddha. Here we accept that they are,

but deny the effectiveness of their teachings and maintain that it is impossible to become rid of disturbing emotions and attitudes by means of their instructions, for example those concerning vipassana — insight meditation.

(15) Proclaiming a false realization of voidness. We commit this downfall if we have not fully realized voidness, yet teach or write about it pretending that we have, because of jealousy of the great masters. It makes no difference whether any students or readers are fooled by our pretense. Nonetheless, they must understand what we explain. If they do not comprehend our discussion, the downfall is incomplete. Although this vow refers to proclaiming false realizations specifically of voidness, it is clear that we need to avoid the same also when teaching bodhichitta or other points of Dharma. There is no fault in teaching voidness before fully realizing it, however, so long as we openly acknowledge this fact and that we are explaining merely from our present level of provisional understanding.

(16) Accepting what has been stolen from the Triple Gem. This downfall is to accept as a gift, offering, salary, reward, fine or bribe anything someone else has stolen or embezzled, either personally or through deputing someone else, from the Buddhas, Dharma or Sangha, including if it belonged only to one, two or three monks or nuns.

(17) Establishing unfair policies. This means to be biased against serious practitioners, because of anger or hostility toward them, and to favor those with lesser attainments, or none at all, because of attachment to them. An example of this downfall is to give most of our time as a teacher to casual private students who can pay high fees and to neglect serious students who can pay us nothing.

(18) Giving up bodhichitta. This is abandoning the wish to attain enlightenment for the benefit of all. Of the two levels of bodhichitta, aspiring and involved, this refers specifically to discarding the former. In doing so, we give up the latter as well.

MAINTAINING VOWS

When people learn of vows such as these, they sometimes feel they are difficult to keep and are afraid to take them. We avoid this kind of intimidation, however, by knowing clearly what vows are. There are two ways to explain them. The first is that vows are an attitude we adopt toward life to restrain ourselves from certain modes of negative conduct. The other is that they are a subtle shape or form we give to our life. In either case, maintaining vows involves mindfulness, alertness and self-control. With mindfulness, we keep our vows in mind throughout each day. With alertness, we maintain watch on our behavior to check if it accords with the vows. If we discover we are transgressing, or about to transgress them, we exercise self-control. In this way, we define and maintain an ethical shape to our life.

Keeping vows and maintaining mindfulness of them are not so alien or difficult to do. If we drive a car, we agree to follow certain rules in order to minimize accidents and maximize safety. These rules shape our driving — we avoid speeding and keep to our side of the road — and outline the most practical and realistic way to reach a destination. After some experience, following the rules becomes so natural that being mindful of them is effortless and never a burden. The same thing happens when maintaining bodhisattva or any other ethical vows.

THE FOUR BINDING FACTORS FOR LOSING VOWS

We lose our vows when we totally drop their shape from our life, or stop trying to maintain it. This is called a root downfall. When it occurs, the only way to regain this ethical shape is to reform our attitude, undertake a purification procedure such as meditation on love and compassion, and retake the vows. From among the eighteen root bodhisattva downfalls, as soon as we develop the state of mind of the ninth or eighteenth — holding a distorted, antagonistic attitude or giving up bodhichitta — we lose, by the very fact of our change of mind, the ethical shape to our life fashioned by bodhisattva vows, and thus we stop all efforts to maintain it. Consequently, we immediately lose all our bodhisattva vows, not just the one we have specifically discarded.

Transgressing the other sixteen bodhisattva vows does not constitute a root downfall unless the attitude accompanying our act contains four binding factors. These factors must be held and maintained from the moment immediately after developing the motivation to break the vow, up until the moment right after completing the act of transgression. The four binding factors are: (1) Not regarding the negative action as detrimental, seeing only advantages to it and undertaking the action with no regrets. (2) Having been in the habit of committing the transgression before, having no wish or intention to refrain now or in the future from repeating it. (3) Delighting in the negative action and undertaking it with joy. And (4) having no sense of honor or face

— which means being shameless and not caring what our teachers or anyone else might think — and thus having no intention of repairing the damage we are doing to ourselves. If all four attitudes do not accompany a transgression of any of the sixteen vows, the bodhisattva shape to our life is still there, as is the effort to maintain it, but they have both become weak. With the sixteen vows, there is a great difference between merely breaking and losing them.

For example, suppose we do not lend somebody one of our books because of attachment to it and miserliness. We see nothing wrong with this — after all, this person might spill coffee on it or not give it back. We have never lent it before and have no intention to change this policy now or in the future. Moreover, when we refuse, we are happy in our decision. We are shameless about saying no, despite the fact that as someone supposedly wishing to bring everyone to enlightenment, how could we not be willing to share any source of knowledge we have? Not embarrassed in the slightest, we do not care what our teacher would think if he or she knew of our action. And we have no intention of doing anything to counterbalance our selfish act. If we have all these attitudes when refusing to lend our book, we have definitely lost the bodhisattva shape to our life. We have totally fallen down in our mahayana training and lost all our bodhisattva vows. On the other hand, if we lack some of these attitudes and do not loan our book, we have merely slackened our efforts to maintain a bodhisattva shape to our life. We still have the vows, but in a weakened form.

WEAKENING VOWS

Transgressing one of the sixteen vows with none of the four binding factors present does not actually weaken our bodhisattva vows. For example, we do not lend our book to someone who asks, but we know it is basically wrong. We do not intend to do this as a policy, we are unhappy about saying no and we are concerned about honor and saving face. We have a valid reason to refuse lending it, such as a pressing need for the book ourselves or we have already promised it to someone else. Our motivation is not attachment to the book or miserliness. We apologize for not being able to lend it now and explain why, assuring the person we shall lend it as soon as possible. To make up the loss, we offer to share our notes. In this way, we fully maintain the bodhisattva form of our life.

We progressively begin to weaken that form and loosen our hold on our vows as we come increasingly under the influence of attachment and miserliness. When all four binding factors are present, we are fully under the sway of these two disturbing emotions, which means we are not engaged any more in overcoming them or realizing our potentials so that we can benefit others. In forsaking the involved level of bodhichitta, we lose our bodhisattva vows which structure that level.

Maintaining the vow to refrain from not sharing Dharma teachings or any other sources of knowledge does not rid us of attachment or miserliness with our books. It merely keeps us from acting under their influence. We may lend our book or, because of an urgent need, not lend it now, but still be attached to it and basically a miser. Vows, however, help in the struggle to exterminate these disturbing emotions and gain liberation from the problems and suffering they bring.

STRENGTHENING WEAKENED VOWS

The first step to repairing our bodhisattva vows if we have weakened or lost them is to openly admit that our transgression was a mistake. If we already felt it was wrong when we actually broke a specific vow, we re-acknowledge our mistake. We then generate four factors that act as opponent forces. These four factors are:

(1) Feeling regret about our action. Regret, whether at the time of transgressing a vow or afterwards, is not the same as guilt. Regret is the wish that we did not have to commit the act we are doing or one we have done. It is the opposite of taking pleasure or later rejoicing in our action. Guilt, on the other hand, is a strong feeling that our action is or was really bad and that we are therefore a truly bad person. Regarding these identities as inherent and eternal, we dwell morbidly on them and do not let go. Guilt, however, is never an appropriate or helpful response to our errors. For instance, if we eat some food that makes us sick, we regret our action — it was a mistake. The fact that we ate that food, however, does not make us inherently bad. We are responsible for our actions and their consequences, but not guilty for them in a condemning sense that deprives us of any feeling of self-worth or dignity.

(2) Promising to try our best not to repeat the mistake. Even if we had such an intention when transgressing the vow, we consciously reaffirm our resolve.

(3) Going back to our basis. This means to reaffirm the safe and positive direction in our life and rededicate our heart to achieving enlightenment for the benefit of all — in other words, revitalizing and fortifying our refuge and aspiring level of bodhichitta.

(4) Undertaking remedial measures to counterbalance our transgression. Such measures include meditating on love and generosity, apologizing for our unkind behavior and engaging in other positive deeds. Since acting constructively requires a sense of honor and face, it counters the lack of these that might have accompanied our negative act. Even if we felt ashamed and embarrassed at the time of the transgression, these positive steps strengthen our self-respect and regard for what our teachers and others might think.

We can see, then, that the bodhisattva vows are in fact quite difficult to lose completely. So long as we sincerely respect and try to keep them as guidelines, we never actually lose them. This is because the four binding factors are never complete even if our disturbing emotions cause us to break a vow. And even in the case of holding a distorted, antagonistic attitude or giving up bodhichitta, if we admit our mistake, muster the opponent forces of regret and so on, and retake the vows, we can recover and resume our path. Therefore, when trying to decide whether or not to take the vows, it is more reasonable to base the decision on an assessment of our ability to sustain continuing effort in trying to keep them as guidelines, rather than our ability to keep them perfectly. It is best, however, never to weaken or lose our vows. Although we are able to walk again after breaking a leg, we may be left with a limp.

SECONDARY BODHISATTVA VOWS

The secondary bodhisattva vows are to restrain from forty-six faulty actions. These faulty actions are divided into seven groups which are detrimental, respectively, to the practice of each of the six far-reaching attitudes and to the ability to benefit others. The six far-reaching attitudes, or "perfections," are generosity, ethical self-discipline, patient tolerance, positive enthusiasm, mental stability and discriminating awareness. An example of one of these faulty actions is not showing respect to our elders. Although such actions hamper progress toward enlightenment, committing them, even with the four binding factors complete, does not constitute a loss of the bodhisattva vows. The fewer number of factors that accompany them, however, and the weaker they are, the less damage we do to our spiritual development along the bodhisattva path. Therefore, if we happen to commit any of these faulty actions, it is best to acknowledge the mistake as soon as possible and apply the opponent powers, as in the case of the root bodhisattva vows.

There are many details to learn about these forty-six, with many exceptions when there is no fault in committing them. These can be studied later while actually engaged in the bodhisattva path. In general, however, the damage to our development of the far-reaching attitudes, and to the benefit we can give to others, depends on the motivation behind our faulty acts. If that motivation is a disturbed state of mind, such as attachment, anger, spite or pride, the damage is much greater than if it is an undisturbed, though detrimental one, such as indifference, laziness or forgetfulness. With indifference, we lack adequate faith or respect in the training to be bothered engaging in it. With laziness, we ignore our practice because we find it more pleasant and easier to do nothing. And lacking mindfulness, we completely forget about our commitment to help others. For many of the forty-six, we are not at fault if we have the intention eventually to eliminate them from our behavior, but our disturbing emotions and attitudes are still too strong to exercise sufficient self-control.

CHAPTER SEVEN
Tantric Vows

OVERVIEW

At a Kalachakra empowerment, or any other anuttarayoga tantra initiation, if we are not yet ready to take tantric vows and commit ourselves to a daily tantric meditational practice, we do not need to be merely observers of the entire procedure. We may take only refuge or, in addition, formally develop the aspiring state of bodhichitta and keep the commitments from that. We may further add only taking the bodhisattva vows. Or, if we have previously taken refuge or both refuge and bodhisattva vows, we may reaffirm and strengthen them. It is not the case that we have only two alternatives: taking either all sets of vows that are offered, or none at all. To receive the empowerment, however, we need to take the full set of tantric vows.

As with bodhisattva vows, there are root and secondary tantric vows which we promise to keep until reaching enlightenment and which continue on our mind-stream into future lives. The Gelug, Kagyü and Sakya traditions confer these vows with any empowerment into one of the two higher classes of tantra — yoga or anuttarayoga — according to their fourfold classification scheme, while the Nyingma tradition confers them with any empowerment into one of the four higher tantra classes — yoga, mahayoga, anuyoga or atiyoga (dzogchen) — according to its sixfold scheme.

Most details from our previous discussion of bodhisattva vows pertain to the tantric vows as well. The root tantric vows are to refrain from fourteen actions which, if committed with four binding factors, constitute a root downfall and precipitate a loss of the tantric vows. Without these vows shaping our life, we cannot gain attainments or realizations from tantric practice. This is because our practice will lack the necessary supporting context. Except for one of the tantric root downfall actions, giving up bodhichitta — the same as with the root bodhisattva vows — a transgression of any of the other thirteen, without the four binding factors being complete, merely weakens the tantric vows. It does not eliminate them from our mind-stream. The secondary tantric vows are to refrain from eight heavy actions which hamper our practice if we commit them. The damage we inflict is proportionate to the number and strength of the binding factors that accompany them. Committing any of the eight even with all four binding factors present, however, does not rid us of our tantric vows.

In the *Kalachakra Tantra,* most of the fourteen root tantric vows are defined more specifically than in the other tantra systems. With Kalachakra empowerment, we promise to keep both the common and the specifically Kalachakra formulations of them. This is relevant advice for practitioners of any of the higher tantra systems. As corroboration, Ngari Panchen, a sixteenth-century master of the Nyingma tradition, has explained that the root tantric vows taken at any dzogchen empowerment are a blend of the common and Kalachakra versions delineated separately in the other three Tibetan lineages. To differentiate clearly the two versions, however, let us follow the commentaries by the Gelug authors Tsongkapa and Kaydrub Norzang-gyatso.

COMMON ROOT TANTRIC VOWS

The fourteen root tantric vows taken in common at empowerments into any system of anuttarayoga tantra are to refrain from the following actions:

(1) Scorning or deriding our vajra master. The object is any teacher from whom we have received either empowerment into any class of tantra, full or partial explanation of any of their texts, or oral guidelines for any of their practices. Scorning or deriding such masters means showing them contempt, faulting or ridiculing them, being disrespectful or impolite, or thinking or saying that their teachings or advice were useless. Having formerly held them in high regard, with honor and respect, we complete this root downfall when we forsake that

attitude, reject them as our teacher and regard them with haughty disdain. Such scornful action, then, is quite different from following the advice in the *Kalachakra Tantra* to keep a respectful distance and no longer study or associate with a tantric master whom we decide is inappropriate for us, not properly qualified or who acts in an unbefitting manner. Scorning or belittling our teachers of only topics that are not unique to tantra, such as compassion or voidness, or who confer upon us only refuge, or either pratimoksha or bodhisattva vows, does not technically constitute this first root tantric downfall. Such action, however, seriously hampers our spiritual progress.

(2) Transgressing the words of an enlightened one. The objects of this action are specifically the contents of an enlightened being's teachings concerning pratimoksha, bodhisattva or tantric vows — whether that person be the Buddha himself or a later great master. Committing this downfall is not simply to transgress a particular vow from one of these sets, having taken it, but to do so with two additional factors present. These are fully acknowledging that the vow derives from someone who has removed all mental obscuration, and trivializing it by thinking or saying that violating it brings no negative consequences. Trivializing and transgressing either injunctions we know an enlightened being has imparted other than those in any of the three sets of vows we have taken, or advice we do not realize an enlightened being has offered, does not constitute a root tantric downfall. It creates obstacles, however, in our spiritual path.

(3) Because of anger, faulting our vajra brothers or sisters. Vajra brothers and sisters are those who hold tantric vows and have received an empowerment into any Buddha-figure system of any class of tantra from the same tantric master. The empowerments do not need to be received at the same time, nor do they need to be into the same system or class of tantra. This downfall occurs when, knowing full well that certain persons are our vajra brothers or sisters, we taunt or verbally abuse them to their face about faults, shortcomings, failings, mistakes, transgressions and so on that they may or may not possess or have committed, and they understand what we say. The motivation must be either hostility, anger or hatred. Pointing out the weaknesses of such persons in a kind manner, with the wish to help them overcome them, is not a fault.

(4) Giving up love for sentient beings. Love is the wish for others to be happy and to have the causes for happiness. The downfall is wishing the opposite for any being, even the worst serial murderer —

namely for someone to be divested of happiness and its causes. The causes for happiness are fully understanding reality and the karmic laws of behavioral cause and effect. We would at least wish a murderer to gain sufficient realization of these points so that he never repeats his atrocities in future lives, and so eventually experiences happiness. Although it is not a root tantric downfall to ignore someone whom we are capable of helping, it is a downfall to think how wonderful it would be if a particular being were never happy.

(5) Giving up bodhichitta. This is the same as the eighteenth bodhisattva root downfall, and amounts to giving up the aspiring state of bodhichitta by thinking we are incapable of attaining Buddhahood for the sake of all beings. Even without the four binding factors present, such a thought voids us of both bodhisattva and tantric vows.

(6) Deriding our own or others' tenets. This is the same as the sixth bodhisattva root downfall, forsaking the holy Dharma, and refers to proclaiming that any of the Buddhist textual teachings are not Buddha's words. "Others' tenets" refer to the sutras of the shravaka, pratyekabuddha or mahayana vehicles, while "our own" are the tantras, also within the mahayana fold.

(7) Disclosing confidential teachings to those who are unripe. Confidential teachings concern actual specific generation or complete stage practices for realizing voidness that are not shared in common with less advanced levels of practice. They include details of specific sadhanas and of techniques for actualizing a greatly blissful deep awareness of voidness with clear light mind. Those unripe for them are people who have not received the appropriate level of empowerment, whether or not they would have faith in these practices if they knew them. Explaining any of these unshared, confidential procedures in sufficient detail to someone whom we know fully well is unripe so that he or she has enough information to attempt the practice, and this person understands the instructions, constitutes the root downfall. The only exception is when there is a great need for explicit explanation, for example to help dispel misinformation and distorted, antagonistic views about tantra. Explaining general tantra theory in a scholarly manner, not sufficient for practice, is likewise not a root downfall. Nevertheless, it weakens the effectiveness of our tantric practice. There is no fault, however, in disclosing confidential teachings to interested observers during a tantric empowerment.

(8) Reviling or abusing our aggregates. Five aggregates, or aggregate factors, constitute each moment of our experience. These five are: forms of physical phenomena such as sights or sounds, feelings of happiness or unhappiness, distinguishing one thing from another, other mental factors such as love or hatred, and types of consciousness such as visual or mental. In brief, our aggregates include our body, mind and emotions. Normally, these aggregate factors are associated with confusion — usually translated as their being "contaminated." With anuttarayoga tantra practice, we remove that confusion about reality and thus totally transform our aggregates. Instead of each moment of experience comprising five factors associated with confusion, each moment eventually becomes a composite of five types of deep awareness dissociated from confusion and which are the underlying natures of the five aggregates. These are the deep awareness that is like a mirror, of the equality of things, of individuality, of how to accomplish purposes and of the sphere of reality. Each of the five is represented by a Buddha-figure, Vairochana and so on. We shall discuss this further in chapter eleven.

An anuttarayoga empowerment plants the seeds to accomplish this transformation. During generation stage practice, we cultivate these seeds by imagining our aggregates to be already in their purified form through visualizing them as their corresponding Buddha-figures. During complete stage practice, we bring these seeds to maturity by engaging our aggregates in special yogic techniques to manifest clear light mind with which to realize the five types of deep awareness.

The eighth root downfall is either to despise our aggregates, thinking them unfit to undergo this transformation, or purposely to damage them because of hatred or contempt. Practicing tantra does not call for a denial or rejection of the sutra view that regarding the body as clean and in the nature of happiness is a form of incorrect consideration. It is quite clear that our body naturally gets dirty and brings us suffering such as sickness and physical pain. Nevertheless, we recognize in tantra that the human body also has a deeper nature, rendering it fit to be used on many levels along the spiritual path to benefit others more fully. When we are unaware of or do not acknowledge that deeper nature, we hate our body, think our mind is no good and consider our emotions as evil. When we hold such attitudes of low self-esteem or, in addition, abuse our body or mind with masochistic behavior, unnecessarily dangerous or punishing life styles, or by polluting them with recreational or narcotic drugs, we commit this tantric root downfall.

(9) Rejecting voidness. Voidness here refers either to the general teaching of the Prajnaparamita sutras that all phenomena, not only persons, are devoid of fantasized and impossible modes of existence, or to the specifically mahayana teachings of the chittamatra or any of the madhyamaka schools concerning phenomena being devoid of a particular fantasized way of existing. To reject such teachings means to doubt, disbelieve or spurn them. No matter which mahayana tenet system we hold while practicing tantra, we need total confidence in its teachings on voidness. Otherwise, if we reject voidness during the course of our practice, or attempt any procedure outside of its context, we may believe, for example, that our visualizations are concretely real. Such misconceptions only perpetuate the sufferings of samsara and may even lead to a mental imbalance. It may be necessary, along the way, to upgrade our tenet system from chittamatra to madhyamaka — or, within madhyamaka, from svatantrika to prasangika — and, in the process, refute the voidness teachings of our former tenet system. Discarding a less sophisticated explanation, however, does not mean leaving ourselves without a correct view of the voidness of all phenomena that is appropriate to our level of understanding.

(10) Being loving toward malevolent people. Malevolent people are those who despise either our personal teacher, spiritual masters in general or the Buddhas, Dharma or the Sangha, or who, in addition, cause harm or damage to any of them. Although it is inappropriate to forsake the wish for such persons to be happy and have the causes for happiness, we commit a root downfall by acting or speaking lovingly toward them. Such action includes being friendly with them, supporting them by buying goods they produce, books that they write, and so on. If we are motivated purely by love and compassion, and possess the means to stop their destructive behavior and transfer them to a more positive state, we would certainly try to do so, even if it means resorting to forceful methods. If we lack these qualifications, however, we incur no fault in simply boycotting such persons.

(11) Not meditating on voidness continually. As with the ninth tantric root downfall, voidness can be understood according to either the chittamatra or madhyamaka systems. Once we gain an understanding of such a view, it is a root downfall to let more than a day and night pass without meditating on it. The usual custom is to meditate

on voidness at least three times during the course of each day and three times each night. We need to continue such practice until we have rid ourselves of all obstacles preventing omniscience — at which point we remain directly mindful of voidness at all times. If we place a limit and think we have meditated enough on voidness before reaching this goal, we can never attain it.

(12) Deterring those with faith. This refers to purposely discouraging people from a particular tantric practice in which they have faith and for which they are fit vessels, with proper empowerment and so forth. If we cause their wish to engage in this practice to end, this root downfall is complete. If they are not yet ready for such practice, however, there is no fault in outlining in a realistic manner what they must master first, even if it might seem daunting. Engaging others like this, taking them and their interests seriously rather than belittling them as incapable, actually boosts their self-confidence to forge ahead.

(13) Not relying properly on the substances that bond us closely to tantric practice. The practice of anuttarayoga tantra includes participating in periodic offering ceremonies known as *tsog pujas*. They involve tasting specially consecrated alcohol and meat. These substances symbolize the aggregates, bodily elements and, in Kalachakra, the energy-winds — ordinarily disturbing factors that have a nature of being able to confer deep awareness when dissociated from confusion and used for the path. The root downfall is to consider such substances nauseating, to refuse them on the grounds of being a teetotaler or a vegetarian, or alternatively, to take them in large quantities with gusto and attachment.

(14) Deriding women. The aim of anuttarayoga tantra is to access and harness clear light mind to apprehend voidness so as to overcome as quickly as possible confusion and its instincts — the principal factors preventing liberation and the full ability to benefit others. A blissful state of awareness is extremely conducive for reaching clear light mind since it draws us into ever deeper, more intense and refined levels of consciousness and energy. Moreover, when blissful awareness reaches the clear light level and focuses on voidness with full understanding, it becomes the most powerful tool for clearing away the instincts of confusion.

During the process of gaining absorbed concentration, we experience increasingly blissful awareness as a result of ridding our mind of dullness and agitation. The same thing happens as we gain ever deeper understanding and realization of voidness, as a result of ridding our mind of disturbing emotions and attitudes. Combining the two, we experience increasingly intense and refined levels of bliss as we gain ever stronger concentration on ever deeper understandings of voidness. In anuttarayoga tantra, men enhance the bliss of their concentrated awareness of voidness even further by relying on women. This practice involves relying on either actual women visualized as female Buddha-figures so as to avoid confusion, or, for those of more refined faculties, merely visualized ones alone. Women enhance their bliss through men in a similar fashion by relying on the fact of their being a woman. Therefore it is a tantric root downfall to belittle, deride, ridicule or consider as inferior a specific woman, women in general or a female Buddha-figure. When we voice low opinion and contempt directly to a woman, with the intention to deride womanhood, and she understands what we say, we complete this root downfall. Although it is improper to deride men, doing so is not a tantric root downfall.

KALACHAKRA ROOT TANTRIC VOWS

The tantric vows conferred at a Kalachakra empowerment include the following more specific formulations of the fourteen root downfalls.

(1) Disturbing the mind of our vajra master. Rather than scorning or deriding our tantric master, here the downfall is to cause a specific insult. Because of a disturbing emotion or attitude, and not for any altruistic purpose, we act or speak in a destructive manner and do not even think to refrain from doing so at any point during our act. When our teacher learns of our conduct and shows displeasure in order to help tame us, this root downfall is complete.

(2) Transgressing our teacher's orders. This is more specific than trivializing and transgressing a vow taught by an enlightened being. Here the downfall is to commit in a hidden fashion one of the ten destructive actions or break one of our vows, after our vajra master has specifically said not to do so. The motivation must be a disturbing emotion or attitude, not some altruistic aim. As with the prior root downfall, we need to recognize our tantric master as a holy being, know fully well that such behavior displeases him or her, and think nothing of engaging in it anyway. Here it is not required that our teacher learns of our misdeed or shows displeasure.

(3) Because of anger, faulting vajra brothers or sisters. This is the same as in the list of common tantric root downfalls.

(4) Giving up love for sentient beings. This is also the same as the corresponding common downfall. The commentary adds the stipulation

that the downfall is only committed when love for a specific being, once lost, does not return for a day and a night. Becoming exasperated and losing love for someone only for a shorter period is not a root downfall.

(5) Giving up bodhichitta. Corresponding to the common tantric root downfall of discarding the wish to attain enlightenment for the benefit of all, here we discard the subtle creative drops that allow us, through Kalachakra complete stage practice, to actualize that enlightenment through an unchanging blissful awareness. Such awareness is reached only upon manifesting clear light mind and generating it as a blissful awareness of voidness. After this most powerful tool is gained, an ever more stable basis for it is built within the central energy-channel by stacking there, through yogic techniques, 21,600 subtle drops — corresponding to the number of Kalachakra hours in a year and breaths in a day. Once stacked, these invisible drops remain fixed in place until attaining enlightenment — which is why the supremely blissful awareness based on them is called "unchanging." Such awareness empowers the understanding of voidness with clear light mind to dispel, in stages, all instincts of confusion and winds of karma in the most efficient manner possible. These drops only disappear upon becoming a Buddha, since at that stage we no longer have the type of physical body that has subtle drops or a central channel.

Whether male or female, whenever we experience the release of energy that accompanies sexual orgasm — regardless of the emission of gross fluids — we lose subtle creative drops, called "bodhichitta" or "jasmine flower drops." These drops form the basis for achieving unchanging blissful awareness. Since such release discards the most efficient means for achieving enlightenment, it is called "giving up bodhichitta." For this root downfall to be complete, however, we need to understand the nature of unchanging blissful awareness, yet release these subtle drops anyway — when there is no special need to do so — through any means, with the wish to attain enlightenment through the bliss of ordinary orgasmic emission. The four binding factors need not accompany this action.

Release of orgasmic energy or fluids in ordinary sexual acts does not constitute a tantric root downfall so long as it is not regarded as something spiritual — specifically, as a means for attaining liberation or enlightenment. However, any experience of orgasmic release, regardless of how we view it, weakens the form we are trying to give to our life with Kalachakra root tantric vows. It counters the purpose of trying to achieve enlightenment as quickly as possible through the Kalachakra technique of unchanging blissful awareness.

It is important to be realistic, not melodramatic about this matter. Taking this vow does not mean having to remain childless or never to have another baby. Nor does it condemn us to stop enjoying ordinary sex or to feel guilty about it. It does mean, however, seeing the bliss of orgasmic emission in the perspective of unchanging blissful awareness, and committing ourselves to revising our values. In short, when we have no control over our orgasmic energies, we stress, with this vow, never to regard the bliss of orgasmic release from ordinary sexual acts as a spiritual experience, as a way to solve all problems, or as a path to enlightenment.

(6) Holding the view of reality in sutra to be inferior to that in tantra. This is more specific than deriding our own or others' tenets by proclaiming that any teaching from the sutra or tantra vehicles does not derive from Buddha's words. Here the downfall is to disparage specifically the voidness explanations found in the Prajnaparamita sutras as inferior to those found in the tantras, although still accepting both as authentic teachings of the Buddha. The motivation must be anger, such as due to sectarian views, and not simply ignorance.

(7) Disclosing confidential teachings to those who are unripe. This is similar to the common downfall except that it refers specifically to teachings on greatly blissful awareness — the most intense of four gradations of joy experienced within the central channel.

(8) Abusing our aggregates. Whereas the common root downfall is either simply reviling or, in addition, abusing our aggregates, here the reference is specifically to the latter. We recognize our aggregates to be in the nature of Buddha-figures and deep awareness, and realize that if we harm them we destroy our blissful awareness and impair our ability to generate more. Yet we still wish to inflict damage or pain on them, and not for the sake of benefiting someone else. This downfall is complete when we actually commit a self-punishing act and experience, as a result, a diminution of whatever level of physical and mental blissful awareness we have attained.

(9) Not having faith in the purity of phenomena. The common tantric root downfall that corresponds to this is rejecting voidness as taught in the chittamatra or any of the madhyamaka schools of tenets. Here the downfall is not only to reject voidness, but to adopt in its stead a fabricated view of reality of our own or someone else's contriving.

This does not include doing this for the sake of others, as when simplifying the voidness teachings to provide beginners with an initial idea.

(10) Having deceitful love. While the common tantric root downfall is being loving toward malevolent people, the Kalachakra downfall is to speak loving words to others while harboring thoughts of malice toward them in our heart. By extension, we commit this downfall by being hypocritical in keeping close bonds with the tantric practices, for example by reciting a daily sadhana text or attending pujas without faith, pretending to be devout, yet hiddenly acting in destructive ways contrary to our pledges.

(11) Conceptualizing about the blissful awareness that is beyond words. The corresponding common tantric root downfall is not meditating on voidness continually. Here, more specifically, we do not accept unchanging blissful awareness when experiencing it in complete stage practice. When this awareness arises, it is a downfall to waver indecisively and not direct it toward continual meditation on voidness.

(12) Faulting pure beings. The common downfall corresponding to this is to destroy people's faith in a particular tantric practice so that they turn from wishing to engage in it. Here, the downfall is to direct discouraging words specifically at meditators accomplished in some tantric practice, faulting and deriding them to their face out of jealousy. This downfall is complete when they understand these words and, as a result, become depressed.

(13) Rejecting the substances that bond us closely to tantric practice, and (14) deriding women. These two are the same as in the list of common tantric root downfalls. The emphasis in the latter, however, is on disparaging women in general.

SELECTED POINTS FROM THE SECONDARY TANTRIC VOWS

The common root tantric vows and those specific to Kalachakra both entail a promise to refrain from eight heavy actions that weaken meditational practice and hamper progress along the anuttarayoga tantra path. As with the forty-six secondary bodhisattva vows, committing any of these eight heavy actions, even with all four binding factors present, does not result in a loss of the tantric vows. Although we can study these secondary tantric vows in detail later, let us discuss a few of their points that often perplex people considering taking the Kalachakra initiation.

One of the secondary tantric vows is not to rely on an unqualified sexual partner. By relying on the bliss and joy that come from union with a woman, without orgasmic release, a male can enhance his blissful discriminating awareness of voidness. A female can accomplish the same while in union with a man, also without orgasmic release, by relying on the fact of her being a woman. Even if we are not at the stage of having some level of blissful awareness of voidness, and even if we lack the ability, gained through mastery of our energy-winds through yogic techniques, to avoid orgasm when in union, nevertheless, as a person having tantric vows, we would naturally admire and sincerely wish to reach these stages. We need to regard our sexual life within this perspective.

For this resolve not to weaken, it is important that our sexual partner share our attitude toward sex. An unqualified partner is someone who does not view sex from a tantric perspective. More specifically, our partner needs to have received empowerment, uphold tantric vows and keep close bonds with the practices. Most important, she or he needs to safeguard purely the fifth Kalachakra root vow and not regard ordinary sex and the bliss of orgasmic release as something spiritual, or as a path to liberation or enlightenment. Furthermore, a potential partner must not have been coerced to enter sexual union — either by force or subtle psychological pressure. An example of the latter is flattering the person as being spiritually advanced, saying that she or he is helping us, as great tantric bodhisattvas, advance on the path and help others more.

When we view sex from a tantric perspective and our sexual partner simply wishes to share love and comfort, we do not need to feel that our two attitudes are mutually exclusive. Enhancing a blissful awareness of voidness through union with a partner is built on a foundation of sharing love and support. However, if our partner is merely obsessed with greed and attachment for carnal pleasure, or views achieving a healthy orgasm as the cure for all psychological disorder, we can easily fall prey to such emotions or ideas, and lose our perspective.

If we already have a sexual partner and become involved with tantra, while she or he is not similarly involved, we certainly would not forsake that partner or pursue extramarital relations with someone holding tantric vows. Nor do we need to convert our partner to Buddhism, or to pressure her or him to take initiation. On the other hand, it is unfair to exploit this person for our spiritual practice or to be dishonest with our feelings and begrudgingly have sex as our duty. The situation calls for kindness, patience and understanding and, above all, a complete lack of pretention about our level of realization and practice. If our partner is receptive, we may gently encourage her or him to overcome shortcomings and realize potentials through effective techniques, not ordinary sex. In such ways as this we try to make our two attitudes toward sex, if not the same, at least more compatible.

Another secondary tantric vow is not to be in union without the three recognitions, which are to distinguish and regard our mind, speech and body as being dissociated from confusion. Without such an attitude, the bliss of union enhances only our desires and attachment, rather than our blissful awareness of voidness. Firstly, our state of mind while in union is a blissful awareness of voidness, on whatever level we can maintain it. We do not harbor ordinary thoughts or worries, for instance about how our sexual performance ranks with other people's. Secondly, our speech labels phenomena as what they conventionally are, not when apprehended by a confused mind, but by one that is a blissful awareness of voidness. With confusion and its attendant attachment, we label sexual organs as desirable objects for gaining the fleeting bliss of orgasmic release. Free of confusion, we label them in a purer manner, as objects that help to enhance a blissful discriminating awareness of voidness. And thirdly, the bodies of ourselves and our partner appear in the form of Buddha-figures which our mind gives rise to while simultaneously maintaining, on a deeper level, a blissful awareness of voidness. Since the mind that generates this appearance is not one of longing desire, this visualization is not at all the same as fantasizing ourselves and our partner as sexy movie stars.

Again it is important to remember that even if we maintain this pure way of regarding our mind, speech and body while in sexual union, if we consider the bliss of orgasmic release experienced within this context as something spiritual, or as a means for achieving liberation or enlightenment, we incur a root tantric downfall. This occurs whether we purposely cause that orgasmic release or experience it unintentionally. Furthermore, even when we visualize our own and our partner's body in a pure form as a Buddha-figure, it is essential not to lose sight of our conventional existence as a person, or that of our partner. We need to remain always sensitive to our own and our partner's feelings and needs. This is pertinent whether our partner shares our attitude and visualization, or is not involved in tantric practice.

The other secondary tantric vow that causes much confusion is not to stay more than seven days among shravakas. In this context, a shravaka is anyone who trivializes or makes fun of tantra. Staying for a long time among such persons discourages us from our path, especially if they are actively hostile toward our meditational practice. There is no fault, however, if we have no choice about whom we live with. It is therefore crucial in such situations — and when living in any non-supportive and unsympathetic environment — to keep our tantric practices and beliefs totally private.

CHAPTER EIGHT

Tamed Behavior and Closely Bonding Practices

MODES OF TAMED BEHAVIOR

Another commitment of the Kalachakra empowerment is to safeguard twenty-five modes of tamed behavior. According to Tsongkapa, this promise is not required by other anuttarayoga tantra systems, whereas Ngari Panchen has asserted that it is common to all highest tantra systems, including dzogchen. In either case, the tamed behavior is to refrain from intentionally committing any of twenty-five negative actions while motivated by longing desire, anger or foolish confusion about either reality or also behavioral cause and effect. A lack of a sense of honor or face must also accompany the action.

The actions are divided into five groups of five. The first group is the same as the laypersons' vows, which are sometimes called the five precepts. The actions to be abandoned are: (1) Taking a life. Since refraining from killing all types of animate beings is specified later in the list of tamed modes of behavior, here taking a life refers to inflicting physical harm on any human or animal. Psychologically tormenting others is also included.

(2) Speaking lies. Especially serious is teaching something untrue that we have contrived. Lying also includes cheating in business, such as setting unfair prices. If others would take undue advantage of our

honesty in negotiating a contract, however, there is no fault in striking a hard bargain so long as our motivation is not greed. Being competitive is not necessarily a disturbing attitude.

(3) Taking what is not given. This is stealing anything, regardless of value, and includes not paying fees or repaying loans. Even using someone else's computer without permission is a form of taking what has not been given.

(4) Inappropriate sexual conduct. Certain times, places and parts of the body are inappropriate for sexual contact since resorting to them usually arises from excessive desire and unwillingness to exercise any restraint in sexual matters. The most inappropriate form of sexual behavior, however, is to have relations with someone else's spouse.

(5) Drinking alcohol. Strictly interpreted, this means not to take even a drop. A similar prohibition extends to narcotics and recreational drugs. Regardless of motivation, consuming alcohol or drugs clouds our judgment, weakens our self-control and often leads to destructive behavior, words or thoughts.

There are several situations in which alcohol can be taken when not motivated by a disturbing emotion. It is not a fault, for example, to taste alcohol at a tsog puja — in fact, to refuse a symbolic taste is a root tantric downfall. Alcohol is also occasionally employed in anuttarayoga tantra to enhance the blissful awareness of voidness, with the same restrictions as the similar use of sexual union. Drinking is never considered a spiritual act or viewed as a path to liberation or enlightenment, and alcohol is employed in the path only when it is accompanied by a yogic mastery of the energy-winds that prevents intoxication and by the full maintenance of a blissful awareness of voidness. This is the meaning of the statement by the nineteenth-century Rimey master Kongtrül that maintaining this mode of tamed behavior does not prohibit tasting alcohol at a tsog puja or using it to enhance our spiritual path so long as we do not become drunk. He was not sanctioning the controlled or moderate consumption of alcohol.

Some people considering taking the Kalachakra initiation are prepared to uphold the other commitments, but find it difficult to promise never to take a drink again. They wonder if this means they cannot take the initiation as a full participant. To answer this question, we may look to the bodhisattva vows and trainings for guidelines. Many of the secondary bodhisattva vows have the stipulation that if we cannot yet stop committing a certain negative action because of strongly disturbing emotions, we avoid a serious fault if we lessen that action and seriously work on ourselves to abandon it in the future. Therefore, some teachers advise potential candidates for the initiation who face this problem that if their attachment is too overwhelming to forsake alcohol yet, they need, with this vow, at least to limit and then steadily decrease their consumption, and not accompany their drinking with the four binding factors. It is important, however, not to rationalize a fondness for alcohol. Even in countries where most people take wine or beer with meals, there is almost always a polite and diplomatic way to decline a drink without offending anyone.

The second of the five groups consists of the five auxiliary destructive actions. (6) Gambling. This includes playing dice, cards, board games and so on, in order to win money, to pass time, or because of competitiveness. Such time-consuming activities divert our constructive energy. There is no fault, however, in playing games for educational purposes or as a way to establish a rapport with children or non-communicative people.

(7) Eating unseemly meat. This is not a promise to be a vegetarian, although such a diet is considered best, if health and circumstances permit. Rather, it is a promise to avoid eating the meat of an animal we either suspect or know was killed especially for our consumption. Such meat is called "unseemly." As with alcohol and sexual union, anuttarayoga practice sometimes employs eating meat, so long as it is not unseemly, to enhance the blissful awareness of voidness by vitalizing our energies. Eating meat, however, is not regarded as a pathway leading to liberation or enlightenment, and it is used only when we have gained some level of blissful awareness of voidness and mastery over our energy-winds so that they do not become heavy because of the meat. Furthermore, when eating meat within this context, it is important to offer prayers for the animal whose life was sacrificed and not to lose sight of the fact that the meat was the flesh of a living being. Like ourselves, it also wished and deserved liberation from suffering.

(8) Reading ignoble words. This refers to reading books, articles or, in a modern context, looking at photos or watching video material that arouses anger or desire when we have no control over these disturbing emotions. Such activities simply increase our delusions. For example, if we read about a villain, we come to hate the person and rejoice when the hero kills him or her. Another formulation of this

negative action is to say anything that comes to our mind, referring specifically to relating stories or talking about topics that incite anger or increase desire.

(9) Making offerings in association with ancestor worship. This does not refer to lighting a candle or placing flowers on a grave in respectful memory of a lost relative, but rather to worshiping spirits. Any form of spirit worship debases our practice. It causes us to lose sight of karma and imagine that liberation from suffering and gaining happiness can come from propitiating nature spirits or spirits of the deceased. The only situations in which making offerings to spirits is appropriate are if it is motivated by compassion to help alleviate their suffering or to placate their wrath if we have caused them offence. It is important to realize, however, that making offerings and prayers for supernatural help can never substitute for constructive action to understand voidness and benefit others.

(10) Following extremist practices, such as sacrificing animals and making blood offerings. Although such types of ritual are rare these days, it is helpful to examine whether we sacrifice the welfare of others in order to get ahead.

The third group comprises five types of murder. (11) Killing cattle, symbolizing animals. People may find it relatively easy to stop hunting and fishing, but much more difficult to stop killing insects. When our automatic reaction to a bug is to squash it, we build up a habit of dealing with every annoyance in life with a violent means. There are often alternative ways to remove insects from our home or fields. And if there are none and we must remove pests for health or economic reasons, it is important not to act with anger or hatred.

(12) Killing children. The commentaries do not explain why children are singled out as a separate category. It may have to do with female infanticide in countries where male offspring are favored. Or, since the ten stages of life outlined in the inner Kalachakra teachings begin as a foetus, the reason may also be to include abortion. There may be certain justifiable reasons for abortion, such as health, but this is a delicate issue and depends on individual circumstances. Often, however, the reason is a disturbing emotion or attitude such as attachment to our own convenience, anger if the pregnancy is the result of rape, or foolish confusion such as considering abortion a means of birth control. Regardless of the motivation, however, abortion after a certain point in the development of the foetal matter is still the taking of a life. If there is no way to avoid taking that life, it is best to try to

ameliorate the results — both the immediate psychological effects as well as long-term karmic ones — by strong thoughts of love and compassion for the unborn child. For example, it may be helpful to acknowledge that life by giving the child a name and honoring him or her with a proper funeral ceremony.

(13) Killing women and (14) killing men. This negative action raises the issue of euthanasia, both of people and pets. There is a great difference between giving someone a lethal injection and withholding medical support to artificially prolong an unsustainable life. From a karmic point of view, the latter choice of allowing for a natural death is preferable, within the context of making the person or creature as comfortable as possible with painkillers.

(15) Destroying representations of Buddha's enlightening body, speech or mind — such as images, texts or reliquary monuments (*stupas*) — or murdering those training in higher ethical self-discipline, concentration or discriminating awareness. If we need to dispose of religious texts for any reason, the usual custom is to burn them with respect.

The fourth group consists of the five types of contempt. (16) Hating friends who benefit the Dharma or the world in general. If we find the methods people employ to help others not very skillful and we become emotionally upset, we soon deny any benefit these persons and methods bring about. This haughty attitude easily leads to egotistic thoughts that only we know best how to benefit others. Such an attitude seriously hampers our ability to help anyone.

(17) Hating leaders or elders worthy of respect. We may not like everyone's personality, but when our personal preferences cloud our discrimination of who is worthy of honor and who is not, we soon lose our ability to discriminate reality.

(18) Hating spiritual masters or Buddhas. The objects include not only our own spiritual masters but extend to other spiritual teachers even if they are not properly qualified. Recognizing mistakes and shortcomings in teachers is not the same as hating them as persons. In some versions, this negative action is showing disrespect for the Buddhas or the Dharma.

(19) Hating members of the Sangha, the highly realized spiritual community. Although the main objects for this negative action are those with straightforward non-conceptual perception of voidness, the Sangha is conventionally represented by the monastic community. Some persons may become monks or nuns for non-spiritual purposes,

yet because of what their robes represent it is inappropriate to show them contempt. In Western circles, the word "sangha" has taken on the meaning of members of a Buddhist center. Enmity within such communities seriously jeopardizes spiritual growth.

(20) Deceiving those who trust us. This negative action includes letting down those who depend on our help, as well as abusing positions of power.

The last set are the five longings, which are to be infatuated with pleasant (21) sights, (22) sounds, (23) fragrances, (24) tastes and (25) tactile or physical sensations. Such infatuations deter our focus from gaining an unchanging blissful awareness of voidness. This is not a promise of asceticism, but rather a pledge to set reasonable limits and exercise self-control, for example at the dining table.

OVERVIEW OF CLOSELY BONDING PRACTICES

In addition to taking vows and, in the case of Kalachakra, promising to keep tamed behavior, we also pledge as an active participant in an anuttarayoga empowerment to maintain certain practices or attitudes that bond us closely to tantra. These are called *samaya* in Sanskrit and *damtsig* in Tibetan, and are sometimes translated as "pledges" or "words of honor." Taking a vow entails promising to restrain from either a naturally destructive action, such as killing, or a form of ethically neutral behavior, such as not meditating on voidness continually, that is detrimental for spiritual advance. Adopting a closely bonding practice, on the other hand, involves pledging to engage in a constructive or ethically neutral act conducive for progress, such as being generous or maintaining chaste behavior.

Kalachakra empowerment calls for adopting a set of auxiliary closely bonding practices common to all anuttarayoga systems and also a set specific to mother tantra — the anuttarayoga tantras that emphasize practices for attaining clear light mind. The common pledges are reformulations or extensions of several of the root tantric vows and modes of tamed behavior, phrased in terms of conduct to adopt rather than actions to avoid. The pledges specific to mother tantra help us to remain on course for achieving blissful awareness of voidness with our clear light mind. There is no need to study their details before receiving empowerment.

The empowerment also requires a pledge to adopt and maintain certain practices that create close bonds with the individual Buddha-family traits. Often translated as "Buddha-families," these traits refer to aspects of Buddha-nature — specifically the aspects of clear light mind as our basis tantra — that allow us to attain enlightenment. As in the case of the aggregates, each is represented in purified form by a Buddha-figure. As with the root tantric vows, there are two versions of these closely bonding practices — one shared in common by all anuttarayoga tantra systems and one specific to Kalachakra. Let us look first at the common practices as explained in the Gelug tradition by Tsongkapa. The other three Tibetan traditions explain them in a similar fashion, with a few minor variations.

COMMON PRACTICES FOR BONDING CLOSELY WITH THE BUDDHA-FAMILY TRAITS

There are nineteen common practices to bond us closely with five Buddha-family traits. To create close bonds with the deep awareness that is like a mirror, represented by the Buddha-figure Vairochana, we take safe direction from (1) the Buddhas, (2) the Dharma and (3) the Sangha. We likewise practice the three types of ethical self-discipline involved in (4) restraining from destructive actions, (5) engaging in constructive ones, such as study and meditation, in order to develop good qualities, and (6) working to benefit others. Many of the Kagyü traditions teach that these practices associated with Vairochana create bonds with the deep awareness of the sphere of reality. In the Nyingma tradition, developing the aspiring and involved levels of bodhichitta substitutes for the first three. Taking safe direction, practicing ethical self-discipline and developing bodhichitta bring ever increasing clarity, as in a mirror, of the sphere of reality of both enlightenment and the course of behavioral cause and effect that leads to it.

Four practices create close bonds with the family trait represented by Ratnasambhava, deep awareness of the equality of things. These are being generous in four ways: giving or being always willing to give (7) material objects or wealth, (8) Dharma teachings or advice, (9) protection from fear, primarily by having equanimity and openness toward others so that they have no fear of being clung to, rejected or ignored by us, and (10) love, the wish for others to be happy and to have the causes for happiness. By giving generously, we gain an ever broader realization of the equality of ourselves and others.

Three practices create close bonds with the deep awareness of the individuality of things, represented by Amitabha. These are upholding the teachings of (11) the three sutra vehicles, (12) the external vehicles of the lower classes of tantra and (13) the confidential vehicles of tantra's higher classes. Upholding all of Buddha's teachings brings an ever deeper appreciation of the individual brilliance and skill of each technique.

Two practices create close bonds with the deep awareness to accomplish things and Amoghasiddhi. These are (14) safeguarding our vows and (15) making offerings. In place of safeguarding vows, the Nyingma tradition substitutes engaging in activities such as pacifying suffering and stimulating others' good qualities. It also divides making offerings into two practices — making offerings in general and offering *tormas*, sculpted cakes made of barley flour and butter. Acting in accordance with vows, engaging in activities like those of a Buddha and making offerings bring ever increasing wisdom and skill to accomplish all purposes.

Finally, four practices create close bonds with Akshobhya and the family trait of the deep awareness of the sphere of reality. Many of the Kagyü systems substitute the deep awareness that is like a mirror. These four practices are (16) keeping a vajra, and the blissful awareness it symbolizes, as our method, (17) keeping a bell, and the discriminating awareness of voidness it represents, as our wisdom, (18) maintaining the *mudra*, or seal of visualizing ourselves as a Buddha-figure couple in union, representing the inseparable union of method and wisdom, and (19) committing ourselves properly to a tantric master. Maintaining a level of awareness that is both blissful and discriminating of voidness and following the instructions of a fully qualified tantric master bring ever fuller realization of the sphere of reality, as clearly as if seen in a mirror.

PRACTICES SPECIFIC TO KALACHAKRA FOR BONDING CLOSELY WITH THE BUDDHA- FAMILY TRAITS

Taking the Kalachakra initiation as a full participant also entails an additional pledge to maintain six practices that create close bonds with six Buddha-family traits. As with the nineteen common pledges, the first five practices create close bonds with the five types of deep awareness, represented by the Buddha-figures Akshobhya, Amoghasiddhi, Ratnasambhava, Amitabha and Vairochana. These are, respectively, taking a life, speaking untrue words, stealing others' wealth, appropriating others' spouses and taking alcohol and meat. The Guhyasamaja system and the higher classes of Nyingma tantra also include these five pledges. Exclusive to Kalachakra, however, is the presentation of a sixth family trait — clear light mind itself, represented by the Buddha-figure Vajrasattva. Not deriding women's sexual organs creates a close bond with this trait. Kalachakra also uniquely presents two levels of meaning for each of the six bonding actions.

On the interpretable level, (1) taking a life means to kill a harmful being, for example a rabid dog that is biting people, when our motivation is solely compassion and there are no other means to stop the damage it is causing. This is similar to one of the secondary bodhisattva vows — not hesitating to commit a destructive action when love and compassion call for it. This type of killing requires the deep awareness of the sphere of reality to differentiate between what is to be accepted and what is to be rejected, as well as the deep awareness that is like a mirror to reflect the full scope of the situation. It also requires the selfless courage, as a budding bodhisattva, to accept whatever painful consequences might follow from our act.

(2) Speaking untrue words means to explain how things appear, which does not accord with how they exist. For example, to help someone to make a difficult decision, such as buying a house, we simplify the variables that need to be taken into account although, in actuality, the issue is far more complex. Speaking deceptive words such as these requires the deep awareness of how to accomplish various aims.

(3) Stealing others' wealth means to take possessions away from people who are miserly with them, in order to help such persons overcome their stinginess, and to give these objects to others in need of them. An example is taxing the rich on luxury items and using the money to feed the poor. Taking what is not readily given arises from the deep awareness of the equality of those in need.

(4) Appropriating others' spouses means to take, under special circumstances, the wives or husbands from people who are overly attached to them, in order to help such persons overcome their dependence. This closely bonding practice does not specifically mean to have an adulterous affair. Even appropriating someone's husband for a few days to help us move house can help his clinging wife to become more self-reliant. Stealing others' spouses is founded on the deep awareness of individuality which singles out a specific person.

(5) Taking alcohol and meat means to use them for special purposes without attachment. Certain medicines have an alcohol base and certain sicknesses, such as hepatitis, call for a diet that includes meat. In order to regain our health and strengthen our body to engage

in meditational practice and serve others, we may need to take these substances even if we would normally avoid them. Taking alcohol and meat in such circumstances requires the deep awareness that is like a mirror to reflect our situation clearly and the deep awareness of the sphere of reality to do what accords with the facts.

(6) Not deriding women's sexual organs is equivalent to the fourteenth root tantric vow — not deriding women. The bliss of union that arises dependent on a woman's sexual organs can enhance the blissful awareness of voidness and bring the mind to more subtle levels so that this blissful awareness is with the clear light mind. In this way, not deriding the female sexual organs creates a close bond with clear light mind.

On the definitive level, the six practices of taking a life and so on are specific techniques cultivated with the Kalachakra complete stage yogas and applied in the central energy-channel at the six main chakras. These practices help to dissolve the subtle energy-winds at these chakras and attain an unchanging blissful awareness of voidness with clear light mind. For example, to take a life means to bind the white subtle creative drops at the crown chakra so as to take the life of the energy-winds of orgasmic release. Since the six chakras are represented by the six Buddha-figures, these practices create close bonds with each.

In the Guhyasamaja and Nyingma systems, the meaning of the first five closely bonding practices of not taking a life and so on corresponds to the definitive level of their meaning in Kalachakra. They are explained as techniques specific to either the Guhyasamaja complete stage or dzogchen.

SIX-SESSION YOGA

If we take Kalachakra or any other anuttarayoga tantra empowerment from within the Gelug tradition as a full participant, we commit ourselves to a daily practice called six-session yoga. Yoga means an "integrating practice" and in six-session yoga we repeat a series of verses and practices six times daily in order to help integrate our life with the nineteen practices that create close bonds with the five Buddha-family traits. Six-session yoga is not the same as a sadhana. Sadhanas contain all the practices that function as causes for being able to proceed to the complete stage, whereas six-session yoga is not as extensive.

The first six-session yoga text was composed in the seventeenth century by the First Panchen Lama. Its fullest versions contain lists of the bodhisattva and tantric vows, as well as the pertinent modes of tamed behavior and closely bonding practices. The recitation also contains verses that help to fulfil the commitments of taking refuge, developing the pledged state of aspiring bodhichitta and following the advice found in *Fifty Stanzas on the Spiritual Teacher* — a text by the late first millennium Indian master Ashvaghosha II, on proper conduct with a tantric master. In this way, daily six-session yoga provides an enduring framework for anuttarayoga tantra practice. We promise to maintain it for the rest of our life.

Although the non-Gelug traditions of Tibetan Buddhism do not have an equivalent to six-session yoga, at anuttarayoga and higher Nyingma tantra empowerments masters from these traditions do confer all the vows and closely bonding practices that this yoga helps us to keep mindful of. Safeguarding vows, however, does not mean simply to recite their particulars. Regardless of which lineage of empowerment we receive, our main responsibility is to shape our life according to our vows and closely bonding practices.

There are several lengths of six-session yoga — abbreviated, full and an expanded version specific to Kalachakra. There is even a version in four lines for emergency use. Regardless of which version we use, we recite it three times during the course of each day and three times each night while generating the appropriate visualizations, thoughts and feelings. We can recite the text either out loud or silently, and in either Tibetan or our own language. Reciting the text in Tibetan without understanding it, however, is hardly beneficial. It is not necessary to recite the same version each time, nor to always follow the same routine. Furthermore, if we have received several anuttarayoga empowerments from within the Gelug tradition, reciting one round of yoga texts six times daily fulfills this commitment for all of them. Thus, from Kalachakra empowerment we need not recite the long Kalachakra version each day, and we do not need to add a second six-session practice if we are already doing one daily.

We may recite a six-session yoga on six separate occasions during the daytime and evening, but most people recite one of the versions three times consecutively each morning before the start of their day and three times consecutively each night before going to sleep. If we do either the full or Kalachakra versions in this manner, only certain verses need to be repeated during the second and third recitations, not the whole text.

If we fall asleep while reciting our evening set, we may add the number of times we missed to our next day's practice. By not waiting until we are about to collapse before we begin, we minimize that danger. If we are rushed in the morning, we may even recite one of the texts six times at night, but it is better to avoid that. Of course, if we are extremely sick and cannot recite anything, there is no fault in missing our six-session practice. However, if we are at all able, we try to maintain the momentum of this practice without any break. It helps keep us on course to enlightenment. Thus, depending on our schedule, we may choose to recite the full version each morning and the abbreviated each night, or vice versa, and occasionally the expanded Kalachakra version on weekends when we have more time.

Since repeating the four-line version three times does not take more than a minute or two, promising to do at least this twice a day is not an outrageous commitment or imposition on our life. If we have time to brush our teeth each morning and evening no matter how busy we are, we have time for a daily six-session practice. In fact, it is much easier to fit into our schedule than anything else because, in an emergency, we can recite it even in our car at a stop light or while waiting to cross the street. We need not be a fanatic requiring a special meditation room, silence and incense in order to remind ourselves of our commitments each day and night through practice of six-session yoga.

CHAPTER NINE
The Preparation Ceremony

KEEPING OUR LEVEL OF PARTICIPATION PRIVATE

By evaluating our preparation for receiving Kalachakra empowerment and our ability to keep the vows and commitments, we can make a realistic decision whether to attend as an active participant or an interested observer. Spiritual practice, especially of tantra, is a private matter, so there is no need to tell anybody about our decision. Tantra, after all, is the secret or confidential vehicle. Keeping our status to ourselves prevents feelings of discomfort or embarrassment, especially if we choose to remain an observer. When red strings and ribbons are passed out during the ritual, we may certainly take them as an observer, so as not to draw undue attention to ourselves. Simply wearing a red string and a ribbon does not signify anything profound. We can drape them on our dog, but that does not mean the animal is taking the initiation.

With this in mind, let us examine the steps of the empowerment so that, regardless of how we attend, we can follow the procedure and gain something from it. Since higher, highest and great vajra master empowerments, as well as subsequent permission, are not always conferred with Kalachakra initiation, we shall look simply at the first level of receiving the empowerment — the preparation ceremony and the seven empowerments of entering like a child.

HOW TO VISUALIZE

From beginning to end, attending a Kalachakra initiation involves visualization. As a participant, we visualize the teacher, the place, ourselves and everyone around us in special ways. As an observer, if we wish to gain the maximum from our experience of attending, we can also do likewise. Therefore, let us begin our discussion by examining what visualization means and how to do it.

First of all, the English word "visualization" does not convey the full meaning of the Sanskrit or Tibetan term, since it connotes working only with the visual sphere. Visualization practice, however, involves sights, sounds, fragrances, tastes, physical sensations, mental feelings such as joy, and senses of who and where we are, what is around us and what is happening. The word "imagination" is perhaps closer to the meaning. Imagining is not just an intellectual activity of trying to bring into focus tiny details of a mental image. It is a process of complete transformation, involving equally the mind, heart, feelings, sense of identity and spatial orientation.

Within the tantric context, successfully imagining something requires two major factors — clarity of appearance and pride. "Pride" means a confident sense or feeling of identity. During the visualizations, we try to feel that our spiritual master and ourselves are actually Buddha-figures, where we are is actually a mandala, and what we picture occurring is actually happening — although of course we must not lose sight of the differences between reality and fantasy. The great meditation masters advise that, in the beginning, it is much more important to have this pride or feeling of actuality than it is to have clarity of details. Although we need at least a vague mental image as a basis for labeling the contents of our visualization, we need not worry about the intricate details. Clarity of them evolves gradually as a function of familiarity and concentration. Worrying about all the fine points that we are asked to imagine during the empowerment only causes us to become overwhelmed, lost and exasperated.

The key for avoiding this kind of frustration is not to worry about the specifics, but to focus instead on creating a deep feeling of our own and our teacher's identity and location. Our spiritual master is the Buddha-figure Kalachakra. Whether or not we can see him or her with twenty-four arms is not the point. The point is the feeling, the recognition of this person as being a totally enlightened being. Furthermore, we are a pure figure ourselves — we are no longer concerned about our weight or our hair. And we are in Kalachakra's symbolic world — we no longer care about the decor or comfort of the room or tent we are in.

THE CLEAR LIGHT BASIS FOR VISUALIZATION

This visualization is not a kind of self-hypnosis or a fantasy-based therapy. The foundation of these visualizations is basis tantra — the everlasting stream of clear light mind. Clear light mind provides each individual being with unbroken continuity from lifetime to lifetime, and into Buddhahood. Like the sky unaffected by clouds, it is unstained by disturbing emotions or attitudes, which fleetingly come and go, temporarily confusing the mind. Thus clear light mind is what allows for enlightenment — the state in which confusion and its instincts are totally absent. Clear light mind is also the foundation for all the abilities and qualities of enlightened beings. It allows for the omniscient mind to be aware of everything and everyone simultaneously, with full understanding, and to have total love and concern for all beings.

Just as we can label "me" onto the aggregate package of our everyday body, thoughts, emotions, attitudes and clear light mind upon which they all rest, and feel that this package is "me," we can do the same with this clear light basis itself as a container or vessel for our future attainment of enlightenment. When receiving or even observing an empowerment into a particular tantric system, we represent this "container aspect" of our clear light mind with the forms of various Buddha-figures that we imagine from that tantric system. We label as "me" our clear light mind with this imagined form, and, on the basis of this valid labeling, we sincerely feel this is actually me. It is not a lie. It is like calling our baby a big boy when he takes his first steps.

Likewise, when we receive empowerment from a tantric master, we are not receiving it from his or her ordinary body, feelings and emotions, but from his or her clear light mind as the basis for enlightenment. We represent this by imagining our teacher also as a Buddha-figure. Even if we do not accept this teacher as our tantric master and simply attend the initiation as an observer, we show our respect and understanding of the proceedings by seeing the teacher in this aspect and form. Similarly, just as we can label the site of the empowerment as an auditorium or circus tent, we can also validly label it as a place of initiation, whether we are a participant or an observer. We represent this by imagining it appearing in the form of a mandala palace.

CONFIRMING OUR ABILITY TO VISUALIZE

Let us prove to ourselves that we are capable of imagining such things and feeling they are actually so, even if we cannot see them in our mind's eye in vivid detail. For example, everyone has the feeling of being a man or a woman, and of being an American, a Swiss or some other nationality. If we take a moment and try to feel who we are, we discover that there is no need to conjure a mental picture or say any words in our mind in order to have a feeling of being a particular gender or nationality. It is this feeling of identity that we employ in holding the "pride" of a visualization, whether we are visualizing ourselves or someone else.

We can boost our feeling of someone's being a nurse, for example, by picturing her wearing a white uniform and holding a thermometer and chart, but this only represents her identity. The important things are our recognition and feeling that she is a nurse. Without them, the white uniform, thermometer and chart have no relevance for us and can be merely a costume for a masquerade ball. Also, if we can picture a refreshing glass of cold orange juice, as well as its taste, when we are hot and thirsty, we have the working materials to be able to picture anything. We just need to develop these skills. It requires merely time, practice and patience. It is not so difficult.

Concerning our location, we can all feel that we are down the street from our office building when we are walking or driving toward it. Whether or not we see it in our mind's eye, we know and feel with deep conviction that our building is there. It is the same with feeling we are outside a mandala palace. Moreover, when we are in front of our building and are late for work, we can have the feeling that our supervisor is sitting inside on the fourth floor waiting for us, whether or not we have a clear picture of him or her in our mind. The same is true with imagining our tantric master inside a mandala on one of the higher floors.

If we think about the room where we are presently located, we can all feel we are in that room. We can be aware of the four walls around us whether or not we can picture them all at once. This is how we imagine being inside a mandala palace. Furthermore, if we are standing in front of the elevator on the ground floor of a multi-storied building, we can feel that there are floors above us, whether or not we can see them in our mind. It is the same with the visualization of being inside a multi-storied mandala, standing on the ground floor. In fact, we can feel all these things at once when we are in front of the elevator

— that we are an employee and late for work, we are downstairs inside our office building and the elevator is taking forever to come, and our supervisor and colleagues are already at work in the office upstairs.

Any details we can add to this scene — such as picturing our co-workers at their desks and ours blatantly empty — enhance our feeling of being late. If we can imagine all the details in living color, the situation becomes so vivid we might even take the stairs. However, even without the details, our recognition and feeling of being late are sufficient to get us moving quickly.

VISUALIZING THE MANDALA AND KEEPING OUR DIRECTIONAL ORIENTATION

To enhance the feeling of being either inside or outside the Kalachakra mandala palace, it is necessary to have at least a rough idea of what it looks like. This magnificent, ornate palace has five stories and is shaped like a square, five-layered wedding cake. Each story is half the size of the one underneath and rests on the center of the floor beneath it. There is a large gateway and entrance porch in the middle of each side. The building is very large, two hundred times our size in length, width and height, and is transparent, made of multi-colored light. In this sense it is reminiscent of a modern office building with walls made entirely of tinted glass.

The empowerment ritual always refers to our position in the palace in terms of the cardinal directions. As this is sometimes confusing, it is helpful to think of a map. If the initiation is taking place in the United States, for example, we could imagine the master conferring it standing in Chicago. We begin the ritual standing on the eastern entrance porch, in New York, facing our teacher in Chicago. To the south is Mexico; to the north, Canada; and to the west, California.

Our teacher, Kalachakra, in the center of the palace has four faces, each of a different color. The floor, ceiling and architectural trimmings of each side of the palace are the same color as his corresponding face. The four faces represent the results of purifying ourselves of the four subtle drops discussed in the internal Kalachakra teachings — the body, speech, mind and deep awareness drops. For this reason, the faces and directional sides of the mandala are the same colors as the seed-syllables that mark the location of these drops in the subtle body. In all tantric systems, we visualize a white *OM*, a red *AH*, and a dark blue or black *HUM* at the forehead, throat and heart respectively to represent body, speech and mind. Kalachakra adds a yellow *HOH* at the navel to represent deep awareness and explains the relation between these syllables and the subtle drops and subtle speech. The color of Kalachakra's faces and the sides of his palace are therefore white, red, black and yellow. This also symbolizes the four elements — water, fire, wind and earth, respectively.

By using simple techniques such as mnemonic devices, we can remember the correlations more easily and thus keep our orientation in the mandala throughout the initiation. The east and main face of Kalachakra are black, standing for mind and wind. New York and the East Coast are often struck with hurricane winds, bringing black clouds and mental stress. The south and right face are red, representing speech and fire. In Mexico, people speak Spanish and the food is hot. The north and left face are white, standing for body and water. Canada is filled with snow and our body feels cold there in winter. The west and rear face are yellow, representing deep awareness and earth. California has deserts of yellow sand and people who are deeply aware of environmental issues.

Thus, with a proper attitude, we do not need to feel that the Kalachakra initiation and all the visualizations are too much for us. The empowerment is an introduction to the experience of expanding our awareness to hold many things at once, with mindfulness and understanding. It "plants seeds" to do this ultimately as a Kalachakra. We need to approach the initiation with confidence, feeling we can open up to this more advanced level of functioning in life. To upgrade our computer, we open it up and insert a new chip or card. Likewise, to upgrade our mind and heart, we open them up to receive new imprints, with confidence that we can digest and incorporate them into our life. Maintaining this conviction throughout the empowerment is the pride of being a proper vessel for Kalachakra.

TEXTUAL TRADITIONS OF THE EMPOWERMENT RITUAL

With these guidelines in mind, let us now discuss the initiation ritual itself. Since in recent times the Kalachakra empowerment is given most frequently by His Holiness the Dalai Lama, we shall outline the procedures from the textual tradition he follows. He confers the Gelug lineage of Kalachakra according to the ritual text composed in the eighteenth century by the Seventh Dalai Lama, which is itself based on Kaydrubjey's fifteenth-century version. The Kagyü and Nyingma lineages follow the ritual composed in the nineteenth century by Kongtrül of the Rimey tradition, which revitalized the Jonang Kalachakra lineage, a minor tradition within Sakya. Sakya masters choose either Kongtrül's text or the fourteenth-century one by Butön. The differences are minor, especially concerning the preparation ceremony and the seven empowerments of entering as a child. In general, the ritual composed by the Seventh Dalai Lama is slightly more elaborate than the other versions. It includes ceremonies for purifying the site where the powdered sand mandala is to be made, meditation dances for claiming that site and making offerings once the mandala is built, and rituals for dismantling the mandala after the empowerment.

ENTERING THE SITE FOR THE CEREMONY

Discounting the rituals for constructing and dismantling the powered sand mandala, the Kalachakra initiation itself has two parts — a preparation ceremony held the first day and the actual empowerment, which spans the next two or three days. To symbolize washing ourselves before coming to the ritual, whether we are a participant or an observer we rinse our mouth with specially consecrated water on the first and second days before entering the site of the empowerment. If the ceremony is outdoors, we discreetly spit out the water onto the grass; if indoors, into a bucket provided as a spittoon. After taking a bath, we do not drink the bath water.

We then imagine going to the black eastern porch of the palace, as if going to New York, and being unable to see what is inside. The palace and surrounding grounds are filled with 722 male and female Buddha-figures. Although the tantric master is manifesting in the form of the entire array, we imagine him or her primarily as the male central figure, Kalachakra. For ease of expression, we shall therefore refer to the master with the masculine pronoun. As the father, he embraces Vishvamata, the Mother of Diversity. Throughout the proceedings he always remains in the center of the fourth floor — counting the ground level where we are standing as the first floor. Whether we are a participant or an observer, we always remain either outside the palace or on the ground floor.

We may note that, as a father and mother in union — the meaning of the Tibetan term *yab-yum* — Kalachakra and Vishvamata symbolize the union of method and wisdom necessary for giving birth to Buddhahood. The tantric image of an embracing couple may have inspired the Swiss psychologist Carl Jung to develop therapeutic techniques for uniting the masculine and feminine aspects of our psyche, but this is not the image's original implication.

Before taking our seat on the eastern porch, we prostrate three times to show respect. If there is no room at the empowerment site to make actual prostrations, or if as an observer we are not in the custom of bowing down to the ground as a sign of respect, we press our palms together and visualize bowing. We then offer a mandala, with the appropriate symbolic hand gesture, as a general request. A mandala is a round, symbolic universe — in this case, not the pure world of a Buddha-figure, but the universe we live in. It makes no difference in what form we conceive that universe. It can be a galaxy, a globe or a flat disc with Mount Meru and four continents. Our offering symbolizes that we are making a gift of the entire world of our life. As a participant, we are willing to give anything and everything in order to gain entrance into the Kalachakra system so as to reach enlightenment through its techniques and be able to help everyone fully as quickly as possible. If we are an observer, we can also offer a mandala with the request to be able to gain inspiration, from attending the empowerment, to foster world peace.

TRANSFORMING OUR SELF-IMAGE WITH THE INNER EMPOWERMENT

Our teacher, Kalachakra, next gives instructions on setting the proper motivation and then confers an inner initiation to transform our appearance and our attitude toward ourselves and what will be happening. Since the symbolic world of Kalachakra is not an ordinary place, we cannot enter it in our usual form. Before entering an operating room, we don an antiseptic gown and take special care to keep ourselves clean. Similarly, as part of the preparation ceremony for entering the mandala, we transform our appearance into a form dissociated from confusion, and adopt and maintain a feeling of purity. We do this by imagining ourselves reborn as the spiritual child of our teacher, Kalachakra, in a simplified form that resembles him and which acts as a basis for growing to maturity. Whether we plan to participate fully in the ensuing empowerments or simply attend as an observer, if we all imagine we transform in this way it fosters an atmosphere of brotherhood and sisterhood. Similar to when the inhabitants of Shambhala joined together in the Kalachakra mandala, this spirit of union contributes to world peace.

The basis for any self-transformation during an empowerment or subsequent practice is voidness. Awareness of voidness withdraws the mind from its usual way of giving rise to ordinary appearances of ourselves and to feelings of pride or identification with those appearances. In that state, we focus on the absence of anyone existing solidly and concretely "out there" who corresponds to our projected image of ourselves, inherently existing as this or that from his or her own side. For example, if our mind ordinarily make us appear to ourselves as fat, ugly and unworthy of love or happiness, and we feel this is truly who we are, we focus on the total absence of any monster corresponding to our paranoid vision of low self-esteem. There is no such person. No one exists in this fantasized and impossible way. If we existed inherently in this manner, from our own side, then everyone should feel this way about us, including our loved ones. This is not so.

Like rebooting our computer, we withdraw our mind from its habitual program — which brings us such anguish and pain — and then reload our basic operating system, namely the pure appearance and feeling of identity of a Kalachakra. In the context of the initiation, the appearance and feeling our mind generates of ourselves as a Kalachakra represents the capacity of our clear light mind to act as a container for developing and using simultaneously all positive qualities. Clear light mind can function in this way on the basis of its being devoid, or purified of all shortcomings and stains. If we attend as an active participant, we imagine this container, during the stages of the ritual, being emptied of fleeting impurities and implanted with seeds for growing these qualities through Kalachakra meditational practice. If we watch as an interested observer, we derive the most benefit if we also readjust our mind in a similar manner during the proceedings. We turn off our usual self-image, with all its attendant worries and fears, and generate instead a view of ourselves as a Kalachakra. We do this on the basis of our clear light mind being a container for positive impressions, gained while watching the empowerment, to inspire us toward future spiritual development. Afterwards, although we do not engage in Kalachakra meditational practice, if we remember to readjust our self-image in this manner whenever a terrible mood arises, we benefit greatly.

During the inner empowerment, we imagine withdrawing to clear light mind and, thinking of voidness, generate ourselves in the form of a spiritual child of our teacher, Kalachakra — a spiritual child of clear light mind. We enact this procedure by imagining the rebirth process as described in the Buddhist systems. First we enter the mouth of our teacher, Kalachakra, like the consciousness of a bardo being entering the mouth of a father, or a meditator's mind entering the mouth of a state of blissful awareness. We melt and, in the form of a white drop of bodhichitta, descend through the center of the father, like a meditator's mind passing down the chakras in the central energy-channel and progressing through levels of awareness that are increasingly blissful and subtle. Through the father's organ, we then enter the womb of the mother, Vishvamata, like a meditator's mind entering clear light. Clear light mind is the "womb for enlightenment," a synonym for the principal aspect of Buddha-nature. In this womb, we focus on voidness and arise in the simplified form of our father — the Buddha-figure Kalachakra — like a meditator's arising, within the context of blissful clear light awareness of voidness, as a devoid form Kalachakra. We have one face, two arms, two legs and are standing upright. Our head, arms and trunk are dark blue, our right leg is red and our left leg white. As a mnemonic device, we can remember the color of our legs by recalling that in English the words "right" and "red" both begin with the letter "r."

GENDER ISSUES IN VISUALIZATION

Although Kalachakra is a male form, there is no need for women to feel uncomfortable visualizing themselves as this Buddha-figure. The male shape in this context has nothing to do with ordinary feelings of masculinity, nor does it imply anything inferior about a female form. Clear light mind, as a basis that continues from one life to another and which is the container for developing all good qualities, is not inherently male or female. In the beginningless cycle of rebirth, no one has exclusively been one or the other. Buddha-figures are beyond the limitations of any gender role. However, since clear light mind is a container for blissful awareness, it is inappropriate to imagine ourselves like some neuter plastic doll. Therefore, when generating an appearance of clear light mind in the form of a figure resembling a human, we include sexual organs. If we generate ourselves as a single figure, these organs must be either male or female, not both. Some anuttarayoga tantra systems, such as Vajrayogini, use the female form. Others, such as Kalachakra, use the male. The pride or feeling of identity maintained in either case is the pride of being clear light mind as a container for growing seeds for enlightenment, not of being masculine or feminine.

CONCLUDING PROCEDURES AND SIGNIFICANCE OF RECEIVING THE INNER EMPOWERMENT

Next, our teacher, Kalachakra, invites all the male and female Buddhas, who enter his mouth and pass into the mother's womb, in the same manner as we have just done, and confer empowerment on us there. This procedure empowers us to be a container for what follows, similar to the way a meditator's remembrance of the Buddhas empowers and inspires him or her, while appearing as a devoid form within the blissful clear light awareness of voidness, to attain Buddhahood. Thus, having arisen as a simple Kalachakra in the mother's womb, we remind ourselves, by thinking of the Buddhas, that we have transformed into a container for planting seeds — a container for reinforcing the Buddha-nature potentials of our clear light mind. Now, as the spiritual child of our teacher, Kalachakra, and clear light mind, we are born from the womb. Emerging from our mother, we return to the black eastern porch outside the palace.

The most essential point with this inner empowerment is to feel that now we have actually become the spiritual child of our teacher, Kalachakra. We need to feel strongly and deeply that we have established a strong link with Kalachakra, both in the form of the specific teacher conferring the empowerment, and on the deepest level, in the form of clear light mind as our Buddha-nature. Although, technically, only the active participants, by virtue of their taking tantric vows later in the initiation ceremony, go on to become vajra brothers and sisters, at this stage both participants and observers join together in one caste. The Tibetan term for caste is also used for Buddha-family trait, and when all family traits are united into one, that singular trait is the clear light mind. Thus, like the people of Shambhala, we discard our petty differences and all return to our common basis, the potential and quality of our clear light mind to act as a container for spiritual growth and attainment. We may decide to pursue a course of Kalachakra practice or to follow another religious or spiritual path. However, by reaffirming that each of us is progressing on the same basis, we assure ourselves and each other that our spiritual programs are all compatible. We can communicate, cooperate and work with each other in harmony and peace. If we continue the proceedings with this strong, deep feeling, it hardly matters whether we imagine that our body is blue, our right leg red and left leg white. Merely visualizing ourselves in this form, but without this feeling, is a trivial experience by comparison.

TAKING VOWS AND TRANSFORMING THE ELEMENTS OF OUR BODY

After receiving the inner empowerment, if we are a participant we request safe direction, the trainings from the pledged state of aspiring bodhichitta, and the bodhisattva vows. If we are an interested observer who wishes to receive the first one, two or all three of these, we make the same request. After our teacher, Kalachakra, sets the appropriate tone for taking these vows by discussing the tantric context of refuge and the bodhisattva path, he confers them upon us as we repeat a short verse three times. Although the empowerment texts explain that the request and conferral of tantric vows follow next, it is customary to postpone this until the next day, during the actual empowerment.

The next step in the preparation ceremony is safeguarding the disciples' inseparable method and wisdom by transforming their six elements into the nature of the six female Buddhas. When the confused mind gives rise to an ordinary self-image, it projects an appearance of it onto the basis of the mind itself and the atoms of the body. Identifying with this self-image, we feel that this is who we inherently are — fat, ugly and unworthy of love or happiness. This is a discordant or "dual" appearance. It does not accord with reality.

In order to remain an open container for the empowerments that follow, we need to purify ourselves of this destructive habit. If our mind no longer focuses on the ordinary elements that comprise our body and mind — earth, water, fire, wind, space and consciousness — its tendency to project onto them the discordant appearance of an ordinary self-image is greatly diminished. It is then easier to maintain concentration on inseparable method and wisdom — blissful awareness inseparably functioning as a discriminating awareness of voidness. Therefore, to help safeguard this concentration so that our mind does not resume its discordant appearance-making, we transform our ordinary elements.

When we dissolve, at the six major chakras of our central energy-channel, all energy-winds that provide our mind with the force to create discordant appearances, we refine our blissful awareness of voidness and bring it to the level of clear light mind. Blissful clear light awareness of voidness gives rise to pure, non-discordant appearances consisting of devoid forms — forms devoid of being based on ordinary atoms. The female Buddhas represent these devoid forms. To symbolize this yogic transformation of the very basis upon which we found our appearance-making, we visualize the six chakras in the

form of discs and seed-syllables of the color appropriate to the six
elements and corresponding female Buddhas. These discs and syllables
represent the replacement of the elements with the female Buddhas.
Visualizing them at the six chakras helps to eventually draw the
energy-winds there.

Since variations of this visualization recur in the Kalachakra initiation and subsequent sadhana practice, it is helpful to create a mnemonic device to remember the colors, elements and locations. The body,
speech, mind and deep awareness subtle drops, located, respectively,
at the forehead, throat, heart and navel, are white, red, black and yellow. As water is white, like snow, it is located at the forehead, like the
body drop. Fire is red and at the throat; wind is black, like a storm
cloud, and at the heart; while earth is yellow and at the navel. Occasionally the positions of earth and wind are reversed, in which case
the elements are arranged in the order of increasing grossness — wind,
fire, water and earth, going from forehead to navel. The space element is green — reminiscent of leaves overhead — and, in either ar-
rangement, is at the crown of the head; while consciousness is blue,
like the depths of a deep ocean of awareness, and is at the pubic region. Similarly, figures in the mandala palace representing space are
green and located at the top of the building, while those representing
consciousness or deep awareness are blue and underneath the structure. Even if we cannot visualize all these colors and details, it is important to feel that we have a pure basis for safeguarding the image of
ourselves as Kalachakra, and that we have deleted the impure basis
— confusing atoms — which would be a foundation for resuming our
negative self-image.

As an observer, it is also helpful to reflect at this point about our
ordinary self-image and how we believe it is who we permanently
are. Although we project our self-image onto the elements of our body
and mind, that image is not identical to those elements and we are not
identical to that image. Our body is old, but we think we are young. In
this way we can start to deconstruct our self-image and our instinctive belief that it is who we truly are.

PURIFYING BODY, SPEECH AND MIND AND
DETERMINING FUTURE ATTAINMENTS

The next step of the preparation ceremony is transforming and elevat-
ing the disciples' body, speech and mind. We do this by visualizing
white, red and black discs and syllables respectively at our forehead,

throat and heart which are the locations of the body, speech and mind subtle drops. The purpose for this is similar to that of the previous step — to help keep the mind from projecting discordant ordinary appearances while awake, dreaming or in deep dreamless sleep. Since we examine our dreams during the night between this ceremony and the actual empowerment, we need this step as a preparation. Variations on this theme of purifying our body, speech and mind recur throughout the initiation and sadhana practice.

The major disciples for the empowerment, as well as a representative of the rest of the audience, now rise and approach the teacher's throne. Holding the twig of a neem tree vertically between their hands, they let it fall onto a tray while reciting a mantra, and then return to their seats. Neem twigs are the traditional toothbrushes of India and symbolize purification. The tray contains the drawing of a simplified mandala with a central region and four sides. The direction of the section in which the twig falls indicates one of the five types of actual attainments the disciples will have the most ease in gaining through Kalachakra practice. These five attainments are the abilities to pacify interference, to stimulate others' good qualities to grow, to exercise a powerful positive influence, to forcefully end dangerous situations, or to achieve the supreme attainment of enlightenment.

Next, blue Karmavajra, the emanated assistant of our teacher, Kalachakra, pours water from a vase into our cupped hands. First we take a small portion to rinse our mouth, and then spit it out. We drink the rest in three sips, to purify our body, speech and mind. Water is distributed similarly during the ritual proceedings of the ensuing days. If we are an observer, we may also accept and drink the water. Imagining that it flushes out negativities and obstacles from our body, speech and mind is beneficial for everyone.

RECEIVING MATERIALS FOR EXAMINING OUR DREAMS

Karmavajra also distributes reeds of kusha grass. That evening, we place a long reed under our mattress, parallel to our body, with the tips toward our head. We place a short one under our pillow, perpendicular to the long one, with the tips away from our face as we sleep on our right side, as Buddha always did. People in India traditionally tie reeds of this grass together to make a broom. Sleeping on top of these reeds symbolically sweeps the mind of impurities so that our dreams that night are especially clear. We examine the dreams we have at the break of dawn for indications of our success at Kalachakra practice. There is no harm, as an observer, if we also take the grass and examine our dreams. It may be good fun, but these dreams do not have any particular spiritual significance. Whether a participant or an observer, it is customary the next day to burn the reeds respectfully or place them among bushes.

Finally, Karmavajra distributes red protection strings to tie around either one of our upper arms. The string signifies Maitreya in two senses of the word. We wear it until either Maitreya, the future Buddha, comes, or we develop pure *maitri*, or love, for all beings. Since Maitreya is not predicted to arrive for several million years, and it may take very long before we develop totally pure love, we wear the string for only a token period of time — usually for the duration of the initiation ceremony — as a reminder to wish all beings to be happy and to have the causes for happiness. Afterwards, we may raise undo notice to ourselves and have to answer endless questions if we exhibit a weathered red string on our arm. To avoid this, we can carry the cord in our wallet or purse if we would like to keep it as a reminder to always be loving. Otherwise, we either burn the string or hang it on a tree. If, as an observer, we find it helpful to tie a sting around our arm to remind us to love our neighbors, we by all means go ahead and do so. If some people in the West tie a string around their finger to remind them of an appointment, we can certainly tie one around our arm to help us stay mindful of love.

Once more we imagine seed-syllables at the locations of our six major chakras in our central energy-channel. The six male Buddhas in the mandala emanate replicas of themselves, which enter and dissolve into these syllables. We then repeat a long mantra to invoke Vajrasattva and elevate our body, speech and mind. Our teacher, Kalachakra, recites verses to inspire and fill us with happiness at our rare and precious opportunity to enter the tantric path. Finally, he gives us the mantra, *OM AH HUM HOH HAM KSHAH* — the six syllables we just imagined on our body — which we repeat after him. In Tibetan the mantra is pronounced "om ah hung ho hankya." He instructs us to repeat this mantra for a short time before going to sleep this night and to examine our dreams upon waking. As an observer, we may also repeat this mantra whenever we feel the need to protect our mind from disturbing thoughts. With this, the preparation ceremony ends.

GENERAL ADVICE

It is difficult to understand and follow everything during an initiation, so we need not worry when we become perplexed or lost. Hardly anyone can manage all the visualizations perfectly. Serious practitioners of any tantric system receive its empowerment repeatedly. The more familiar we become with the ritual, the more fully we are able to participate in its visualizations. We try our best to follow on our own level, without worrying about it or feeling inadequate.

My late teacher, Tsenzhab Serkong Rinpochey, gave an extremely useful guideline for tantric visualization practice. Empowerments, sadhanas, pujas and other tantric procedures are like a motion picture. Each frame and scene of a movie runs for only its slated time. It then passes and the next scene appears. We do not try to superimpose every frame of the movie and show them all at the same time. Similarly, we maintain specific visualizations of various Buddha-figures, discs, syllables and so forth at different parts of our body only for the short period of the step of the empowerment that calls for them. When the scene changes and the movie goes on, we drop that visualization and proceed to the next one. If we miss a scene or are unable to keep up, we simply forget about it and do not worry. We go on to the next scene. Otherwise, the movie gets tangled in the projector and cannot play at all. This is useful advice for our lives as well. Life runs more smoothly if we let its scenes pass like in a movie and do not hold on to them with guilt or recrimination.

CHAPTER TEN

The First Day of the Actual Empowerment

PRELIMINARY STEPS

The actual empowerment begins with the disciples rinsing their mouths and prostrating, as the day before. Whether a participant or an observer, we still imagine ourselves as a simple Kalachakra on the black eastern porch of the mandala palace, and our teacher as a full Kalachakra. The teacher, Kalachakra, begins by discussing how to analyze the dreams of the night before. Dreams of spiritual masters, the mandala, washing ourselves, putting on new clothes, walking uphill or entering a temple are auspicious, indicating future success with the practice. Dreams of being beaten, going downhill, walking backwards or of blood-red flowers, signifying injury, are just the opposite. Being proud of favorable signs or depressed at ominous ones causes interference to our practice. Therefore, regardless of our dream, we need to remind ourselves of voidness and dependent arising. Success or failure in spiritual practice do not exist inherently, pre-ordained and totally fixed, but arise dependently on the efforts we make. To dispel interference, our teacher, Kalachakra, offers a torma — a ritual cake. This offering symbolizes the power of the understanding of voidness to dispel superstition and confusion. Whether we are a participant or an observer, we need to flush our mind of foolish thoughts.

If, by chance, we missed the preparation ceremony and begin the empowerment here, we do not face any major problems. We shall be generated once more as a Buddha-figure and repeat many of the procedures. We missed, however, the movie scene of receiving kusha grass and examining our dreams. As these are not essential parts of the empowerment procedure, we need not fret or try to rewind the film by asking for some kusha grass now. And although we lack a red string around our arm, we remain mindful, as best we can, of love for all beings.

The ceremony continues as we offer a mandala and recite mantras, rejoicing at the opportunity to receive empowerment. Again, we request safe direction, the trainings from the pledged state of aspiring bodhichitta, and bodhisattva vows. Karmavajra gives ritual garments to a few of the main disciples, and they put them on as aids for maintaining mindfulness of appearing in the form of a Buddha-figure. Since the main point is visualizing and feeling that we do not appear in our ordinary form, we need not feel disappointed if we do not receive a new set of clothes. Everyone, however, receives a red ribbon and a flower. We drape the ribbon across our forehead as a symbolic blindfold, and keep the flower safely in our lap or pocket for later use in the ritual. As mentioned before, there is no harm if, as an observer, we also take a ribbon and a flower.

The blindfold is worn during the first part of the empowerment ritual, when we are not yet authorized to see the mandala. During the initial steps we remain, in the language of the ritual, outside the curtain over the doorway, which means on the eastern porch outside the walls of the palace. During the rest of this phase, we are inside the curtain, meaning within the building. At the appropriate moment, we remove the blindfold and are able to see all the details of the mandala palace. The visualization task becomes more challenging from this point onward, as the actual empowerments begin. We need to keep our main emphasis, however, on the feeling of who and where we are and what is happening to us there.

VISUALIZING OURSELVES AS A COUPLE AND TAKING VOWS

After putting on a blindfold, and repeating the procedures of the day before of tossing the twig of a neem tree and receiving purifying water to sip, we imagine ourselves, if we are a participant, transformed from a single Buddha-figure Kalachakra into a Kalachakra embracing a female partner. This partner has one face, two arms, two legs, is standing, and depending on the ritual tradition is either entirely blue or yellow. In general, the female member of the principal couple is

Vishvamata, who is normally yellow. Closely associated with the couple are ten female figures, called "powerful ladies" (*shakti*), who represent the ten far-reaching attitudes, or "perfections." Eight of them encircle the couple in the mandala, while two are merged inseparably with Vishvamata. Although any of the ten may substitute for Vishvamata, the blue figure representing far-reaching discriminating awareness, or the "perfection of wisdom," Prajnaparamita, most frequently does.

Since, as an initiate, we visualize ourselves as one or another couple throughout most of the rest of the empowerment, it is important to know how to perform this type of visualization. It is not the case that male participants imagine they are the male member of the couple while women imagine they are the female, or that we picture ourselves in union with some other person. Each of us are both members of the couple at once, though the visual orientation is from the perspective of the male member. Feelings of masculinity, femininity or an androgynous union of both, are totally irrelevant.

If we are married or living with a partner, we are familiar with the feeling of being a couple. If this is a healthy relation, we do not merge into or lose ourselves in the other person, but maintain our individual perspective. We use a similar type of feeling here, in this context, to imagine we are a Kalachakra couple, while maintaining our perspective as the male member.

The visualization of being a couple forever in union signifies the mind inseparably coupling method and wisdom. On one level, method and wisdom refer to compassion and discriminating awareness of voidness; on another level, they refer to blissful awareness and again discriminating awareness of voidness. On yet another level, they refer to unchanging blissful awareness of voidness and devoid forms. Imagining ourselves a couple, then, means to feel we embody three levels of a perfect blend — of positive feelings toward others and understanding reality, of joy and wisdom, and of mind and body. Furthermore, just as an ordinary self-image of being a couple is psychologically supportive — filling us with feelings of self-confidence, well-being and joy — such an image, when dissociated from confusion, acts as an extremely conducive foundation and container for cultivating blissful awareness of voidness.

Someone once asked Tsenzhab Serkong Rinpochey how to visualize ourselves as a couple when walking, prostrating or engaging in any routine activity. Doesn't the partner get in the way? Rinpochey replied that, in a certain way, imagining that we are conducting our daily life in union with a partner is like wearing clothes. Whether we are sitting, walking or cleaning house, we have our clothes on. We know and feel we are dressed. Our clothing becomes so much a part of us, accompanying us no matter where we go or what we do, that we do not think about it as something separate. Throughout the day we consider ourselves the whole package of our body and clothes. Likewise, when imagining being a Kalachakra couple, we do not consider the male and female members separately. Nor do we particularly focus on the female member walking to various sections of the mandala and receiving empowerment — except inasmuch as we remain mindful of the wisdom of voidness she represents. When trying to understand how to work with a visualization of being a couple, we need to remember that the practice deals with a self-image, not an actual relationship with another person. The protocol of interpersonal relations does not pertain.

If we are attending the empowerment as an observer and wish to visualize, we remain in single form throughout the rest of the ceremony. This is sufficient to block our ordinary view of ourselves and to keep us mindful of our clear light mind as a container for receiving impressions of the world of Kalachakra. Such visualization helps keep our mind and heart open to derive the most benefit from the experience.

Our teacher, Kalachakra, now asks the disciples their family trait — whether it is hinayana or mahayana — and what they seek. As a participant, we answer we are fortunate beings with mahayana Buddha-nature, seeking the greatly blissful awareness of Buddhahood for the sake of all. We then take once more safe direction and the bodhisattva vows. As an observer, we may also take them once more, if we wish. Only full participants, however, take the next step, which is requesting and taking the tantric vows and promising to uphold the twenty-five modes of tamed behavior. Observers just watch and bear witness.

THE YOGA ENCOMPASSING EVERYTHING

The next procedure, the yoga encompassing everything, reconfirms two of the most basic prerequisites for tantric practice — conventional and deepest bodhichitta. Bodhichitta is a heart or mind that is aimed at *bodhi*, the ultimate state. Holding this mind on the conventional or "relative" level is to aim at enlightenment with the intention to achieve it and to benefit all beings by means of that attainment. Holding it on the deepest or "ultimate" level is to focus on voidness, the nature of enlightenment and of all beings and all phenomena. Enlightenment is devoid of existing in any fantasized, impossible manner. All the abilities we gain with its attainment arise dependently as a result of building up bountiful stores of positive potential and deep awareness through relying on other beings and the various aspects of our Buddha-nature.

In one way, we can think of bodhichitta as an expanding heart and mind. When we cultivate it on a conventional level, we expand our heart to encompass all others and the goal of the state of enlightenment to help them fully. When we develop deepest-level bodhichitta, we expand our mind to encompass the voidness of all phenomena. With the yoga encompassing everything, we expand our heart and mind at this point, just before entering the mandala palace, with these two bodhichittas. We represent them as a white moon disc lying flat at our heart and a white vajra scepter standing upright on it. A replica, from a similar moon and vajra at the heart of our teacher, Kalachakra, dissolves into them, making their realization firm and stable. Together with our visualization, the feeling of being a Kalachakra couple and the sets of vows, these two bodhichittas shape the container of our clear light mind to receive empowerment. As an observer, we also benefit greatly if we generate them at this point. Whether a participant or an observer, we need to maintain the two bodhichittas as an integral part of our attitude throughout the rest of the proceedings. However, we stop visualizing the moon and vajra at our heart when the scene shifts to the next stage of the ritual.

CONFIDENTIALITY

Before and after entering the mandala, we make a pledge of confidentiality. This completes the process of molding our clear light mind into the most fitting container for empowerment. If a container is leak-proof, it holds whatever is put inside without losing a drop. Likewise, by keeping private the empowerment procedures and our subsequent practice of tantra, we maintain their effectiveness. Secrecy is emphasized in tantra not in order to hide something dirty or bad, but because visualizations and other procedures for innermost spiritual transformation, when publicized, lose their potency. It is totally devastating

to our meditation practice if we tell people we are visualizing ourselves as a deity with four faces and twenty-four arms, and they make
fun of us or accuse us of being crazy. We become defensive or start
doubting ourselves, and our meditation falls flat on its face.

For this reason, we need to keep to ourselves whatever tantric
methods and practices we follow. If people inquire about our meditation, it is best to reply in general terms, explaining, for example, that
we are working on our self-image, trying to develop a more positive
attitude and training our imagination. It is best to keep our answer
simple. Nobody needs to know the specifics of the method we are
following or what we are visualizing. One of the secondary tantric
vows, in fact, is not to make a show of confidential matters. For this
reason, it is improper to display paintings or statues of tantric figures
with fearsome faces and in sexual embrace in prominent places in our
home where anybody can see them and ask embarrassing questions
or make lewd remarks. The more private our practice, the more precious it becomes. Also, if we explain what we are doing to people who
are not sufficiently broad-minded to understand, we may cause them
to develop strange ideas. Silence is often the best way to avoid confusion and misunderstanding. As an observer, it is also important to
keep our experiences at the empowerment private and not to discuss
them with people who would misconstrue them.

ENTERING THE MANDALA BLINDFOLDED

With the container of our clear light mind now fully prepared, we
enter the mandala palace through the black eastern doorway. Blindfolded and led by Kalachakra's assistant, we circumambulate clockwise three times to show respect. We do this along a corridor on the
ground floor, between the wall and a high, broad platform on which
many figures sit or stand. We then offer six sets of three prostrations,
one round each to the male heads of the five Buddha-families — sometimes called the five "dhyani Buddhas" — and then one round to our
teacher, Kalachakra himself. The five male Buddhas sit on the fourth
floor of the mandala. The color of the side where each sits corresponds
to the color of his body and the element associated with his family
trait. Akshobhya, however, is merged with the main central figure.
We prostrate to the five male Buddhas in the wide entrance hall in the
middle of the side of the mandala corresponding to each. The prostrations to Akshobhya and to our teacher, Kalachakra, are offered in the

black eastern entrance hall. For each round, we transform, as a participant, into a simple form of the male Buddha to whom we are prostrating. After each round, we imagine that a replica of the appropriate Buddha comes from the fourth floor and dissolves into us.

The order, colors and directional locations of the male Buddhas in Kalachakra are different from those in other anuttarayoga tantra systems. Symmetry is stupid. Kalachakra assigns the dhyani Buddhas the color and direction of their associated element, and prostrations to them are offered in the order of increasing grossness of their elements. This is why the Kalachakra ritual always lists directions in the order of center, east, south, north and west. If we keep the map of North America in mind, we do not get lost. Prostrating in black New York first to green Akshobhya associated with space and then black Amoghasiddhi corresponding to wind, we pass clockwise along the corridor to red Mexico and prostrate to red Ratnasambhava connected with fire. Always circling clockwise and remaining on the ground floor, we proceed to white Canada to pay our respects to white Amitabha associated with water, and then all the way round to yellow California for yellow Vairochana corresponding to earth. Remaining as a yellow Vairochana, we circle back to black New York and offer prostration to our teacher, Kalachakra.

If it is all too fast and we cannot follow, there is no need to panic. The main feeling to generate and focus upon is that we are greeting, with a show of deep respect, the heads of the families who live in the palace. When a replica of each of these figures dissolves into us, we feel welcomed and inspired to stay. If we wish to be polite as an observer, we also imagine offering prostration or any other appropriate sign of respect, while remaining as a simple Kalachakra.

Before proceeding, our teacher, Kalachakra, once more reminds us of our pledge to keep confidentiality and especially to follow the most important rule of the house, never to disparage him. This is the first root tantric vow. It is extremely important, because if, as disciples, we think that our spiritual master does not know what he is talking about, we cannot possibly have any confidence in what he teaches. The time to examine the suitability of a tantric master is before receiving empowerment, not afterwards. As Tsenzhab Serkong Rinpochey used to say, do not act like a madman who runs out on the ice of a frozen lake and then turns around and taps with a stick to see if it will hold him. Our teacher, Kalachakra, confirms that we have examined him thoroughly beforehand and that we are entering the empowerment fully aware of what we are doing. As a full participant, we need to take seriously the steps we are about to take. As an observer, we also need a sober attitude. We are not attending in order to judge or criticize the teacher, but to gain an impression of tantra and, specifically, of Kalachakra because of our sincere interest.

MAKING OUR VISUALIZATION MORE FIRM

In general, we set the stage for receiving empowerment by first visualizing ourselves in the form of what is usually translated as a "commitment being." This is a form which bonds us closely with a Buddha-figure. It acts as a container for receiving the empowerment. The tantric master then calls forth deep awareness beings — usually translated as "wisdom beings" — and we imagine they merge with our visualization to make it more firm. The Kalachakra system provides a clear explanation of the mechanism involved.

As we discussed in relation to internal Kalachakra, the breath passes predominantly through one nostril or the other during the course of a day. During the shift from one nostril to the other, however, a certain number of breaths pass evenly through both. These are known as deep awareness breaths and they enter the central energy-channel. Normally, no other breaths pass through this channel. Complete stage practice transforms all breaths and energy-winds into deep awareness ones through using special yogic techniques to draw them into the central channel. By dissolving them there at the center of the six main chakras, we manifest clear light mind, which we then use for generating deep awareness of voidness.

The breaths and energy-winds that enter the central channel are called deep awareness breaths because they lead to this deep awareness of voidness. They are represented by Vajravega, the forceful form of Kalachakra. The visualization of drawing in and merging deep awareness beings with closely bonding visualized ones symbolizes bringing the deep awareness breaths and energies into the central channel and dissolving them there for gaining deep awareness of voidness. Clear light deep awareness of voidness gives rise to devoid form Kalachakras. Since devoid forms, compared to mere visualizations, are far more stable containers for receiving empowerment and attaining enlightenment, the imaginative merging of wisdom beings with commitment ones reinforces and strengthens our capacity to contain the initiations that will follow.

INVOKING DEEP AWARENESS BEINGS

The next procedure, invoking deep awareness beings, appropriately begins by transforming ourselves, via meditation on voidness, into the visualized form of a blue Vajravega. We only make this transformation if we are a participant. Vajravega looks like the full form of Kalachakra, except that his front face is ferocious and he has two extra arms, making a total of twenty-six. We imagine appropriate element and planet discs at our navel, heart, throat and forehead in the color of the subtle drop found at each spot — yellow, black, red and white. Lights shine forth from the seed-syllables marking our four planet discs and radiate as well from the heart of our teacher, Kalachakra. They return, bringing back yellow, black, red and white Buddha-figures — called Vajra Deep Awareness, Vajra Mind, Vajra Speech and Vajra Body. These figures dissolve into the syllables at the location of their corresponding drops in our body, symbolizing the drawing in of deep awareness breaths and winds into our central channel and dissolving them at the chakras associated with the four subtle drops.

This is the first place at which any noticeable variations occur in the different Kalachakra initiation rites. Butön makes no mention of lights shining forth from the four spots on our body, and describes them only coming from the heart of the teacher, Kalachakra. Kongtrül follows Butön on this point and, in addition, makes no mention of any visualizations at the navel for Vajra Deep Awareness. We can see from this example that the differences among the initiation traditions are indeed very slight. Most of the differences are simply condensations of the procedures elaborated in the Seventh Dalai Lama's text. Tantric masters conferring Kalachakra initiation according to such abbreviated texts may or may not add the fuller detail, depending on circumstances.

In all versions of the ritual we continue this step of invoking deep awareness beings by visualizing wind and fire discs beneath our feet. The ritual uses these in a sequence of events designed to simulate the process of lighting *tummo* — the inner flame at the navel chakra which, when lit, causes the energy-winds to pour into the central-channel. A rain of deep awareness beings in the form of Kalachakras and Vajravegas then descends and melts into our body as our teacher, Kalachakra, rings his bell. To confirm the dissolution of deep awareness winds into our six chakras, we imagine each chakra marked with a seed-syllable of the appropriate color.

The sequence of visualizations for this step is quite difficult to execute unless we have considerable meditation experience. If we cannot keep up, the main feeling to focus on is of a rain of figures and energy descending upon and dissolving into our very core. With this rain, we feel that all of our energies collect and absorb as well. As a result, our form as a Buddha-figure becomes fortified and more capable of containing the empowerments that follow. We discard any feelings we might have had of our form being merely a convenient pretense. Instead, we feel strong, vital and, in a sense, more authentic, like soil that has become moist and fertile after a spring shower. As an observer, we appreciate and bask in the vibrancy of this process, but without participating in it, like someone sitting on a covered porch and smelling the freshness that follows a rain.

FINAL PROCEDURES BEFORE RECEIVING THE MAIN EMPOWERMENTS

After lifting our blindfold for a moment to note what color we see first, indicative of specific future attainments, we circumambulate the mandala three times clockwise once more, through the same corridor as before. Our teacher, Kalachakra, then assumes the form of his assistant and comes from the fourth floor down to where we are standing, as a participant, in the form of Vajravega in the black eastern entrance hall on the ground floor. To symbolize this, the master conferring the empowerment descends from the throne and stands in front of the powdered sand mandala. There he recites verses, known as words of truth, so that the disciples receive a clear indication of the Buddha-family trait with which they have the strongest affinity. As an observer, we stand watching this at the rear of the same hall, in the form of a simple Kalachakra.

The main disciples and a representative of the others then come forward and with both hands hold the flower they were given at the beginning of the day above a drawing of a simplified mandala placed on a tray. They let the flower drop, while reciting a mantra, and then return to their seats. The section of the mandala in which it lands indicates their closest Buddha-family trait. In the future, from among the nineteen closely bonding practices maintained through daily six-session yoga, we especially emphasize, as a practitioner, those practices that bond us closely with this trait. For example, if the flower falls in the southern quarter, we put special effort into the four types of generosity that create close bonds with the deep awareness of the equality of everyone. We make the smoothest progress to enlightenment through that path. We also receive, as a disciple, a confidential name, which is a variation of the name of the principal male figure of this Buddha-family. In our example, from Ratnasambhava we would obtain the name Ratnavajra.

This confidential name is used only when we need to repeat it when taking or reaffirming our vows during our next Kalachakra empowerment and in our sadhana practice up to that time. It is not used in any other context. Since most tantric practitioners receive empowerment many times, they discover new affiliations and receive new names on each occasion. Therefore the ones obtained at any specific empowerment are not regarded permanent, but just indicative of our present needs. With each new Kalachakra initiation, we change our name and emphasize other closely bonding practices if the flower falls in a different quadrant from before.

Our teacher, Kalachakra, then returns our flower and we place it on the top of our head. From the circumstance of the sensation of the flower touching our head, we experience blissful awareness of voidness. In the next chapter, we shall discuss how to generate this awareness and what, as an observer, we can best feel at this and similar points during the rest of the empowerment. Our teacher, Kalachakra, now returns to the fourth floor of the mandala palace and sits once more on his throne. We remove our blindfold and imagine seeing clearly all the details of the mandala world. Our teacher, Kalachakra, introduces and describes all the figures and we recite certain words to bond closely with them all. The first day of the actual empowerment usually ends here.

CHAPTER ELEVEN

The Second Day of the Actual Empowerment

THEORETICAL BASIS FOR EMPOWERMENT

In general, there are three phases of empowerment that occur along the path to enlightenment. The first — causal empowerment that brings maturation — is conferred with such procedures as the Kalachakra initiation. It purifies the grossest levels of obstacles and plants seeds that ripen in the form of successful generation and complete stage practice. In this way, it acts as a cause for the future attainment of enlightenment. The second phase of empowerment — pathway empowerment that brings liberation — occurs with the progressive mastery of the complete stage practices. Since mastery of each step of the complete stage actually eliminates and frees us from obstacles, it empowers the attainments that follow, bringing us ever closer to enlightenment. The third phase of empowerment — the resultant empowerment of being liberated — is the actual attainment of enlightenment. Enlightenment totally eliminates all obstacles preventing omniscience and empowers us to benefit others in infinite ways. Furthermore, there is empowerment from our foundation. This refers to clear light mind which empowers each of these three phases. Within Tibetan Buddhism, it is discussed most fully in the context of dzogchen, the great completeness.

Clear light mind has never been stained by any obstacles or blocks. Naturally free of them, it is only temporarily obscured by winds of karma and disturbing emotions and attitudes. In this sense, the natural purity of clear light mind empowers the removal of all fleeting stains. If obscuration were the nature of clear light mind, it could never be purified and enlightenment could never be attained. Furthermore, all qualities of a Buddha are complete in clear light mind, although they do not function when the mind is obscured. Put simply, these qualities are complete in the form of traces or potentials, known as Buddha-nature — factors that allow for enlightenment. Thus clear light mind empowers all the qualities that are attained with Buddhahood.

During the initiations on the second day, we are asked, as a participant, to feel that our mind-stream — the continuity of our clear light mind — has been purified of certain obstacles and implanted with certain seeds. We need to comprehend what this actually means in order to feel something meaningful during the ceremony. The key is understanding the interdependent relation between causal and foundational empowerment. Let us first discuss this on the level that is common to all anuttarayoga systems, including Kalachakra.

THE RELATION BETWEEN BUDDHA-NATURE AND EMPOWERMENT FOR PURIFYING OBSTACLES

Each factor of our Buddha-nature, for example the deep awareness of the equality of everyone, when associated with confusion generates a component part of our ordinary experience — in this case the aggregate package of our feelings of happiness or sadness. Confused about the actual equal nature of ourselves and all others, and consequently lacking equanimity, we act with pride and miserliness. Thinking ourselves superior, we are unwilling to share. This selfishness clouds and obscures the underlying awareness of equality with which we consider ourselves and others at the same time. Lacking balance, we experience ever changing moods — the aggregate of feelings.

Purifying this aggregate with causal empowerment does not mean that it is cleansed forever of confusion or of the pride and miserliness that confusion generates. Rather, the causal empowerment brings us to the aspect of Buddha-nature that is the basis of this aggregate — our deep awareness of equality. This is represented by a Buddha-figure from the mandala — in this case, Ratnasambhava. By reaffirming that our aggregate of feelings is in the nature of Ratnasambhava, we reconfirm its nature as deep awareness of equality. The combination of causal and foundational empowerment creates the conviction that through generation and complete stage practice, and eventually pathway and resultant empowerment, we remove forever the obstacles from that deep awareness which have been causing it to remain as an aggregate of feelings associated with confusion.

CAUSAL AND FOUNDATIONAL SEEDS

Planting a seed, with causal empowerment, for this deep awareness to function fully does not place something alien on our clear light mindstream. Deep awareness of equality is part of everyone's Buddhanature. It is a foundational seed which is already there. We know of its presence because it already functions to a limited extent — everyone is capable of regarding several items as equally belonging to the same category, such as several shirts in a store being equally our size. The seed that causal empowerment implants reinforces this foundational seed so that, together, they give rise to pathway and resultant deep awareness.

Causal and foundational seeds function together through one of two mechanisms. This is because there are two types of foundational seed or Buddha-nature — abiding and evolving. Both have been an integral part of the mind-stream without beginning — in the former case in the same abiding aspect, in the latter as antecedent forms that evolve — and both are factors that allow for the attainment of the various bodies of a Buddha. Abiding factors continue into Buddhahood in purified form, as Buddha-bodies. Evolving factors transform into Buddha-bodies, but are no longer present with enlightenment. Like an actual seed, they are no longer present when the fully grown plant has matured.

Although there is much debate over this point, many masters consider the five types of deep awareness to be abiding Buddha-natures. This is because they continue into Buddhahood in purified form as the five types of deep awareness of a Buddha. Implanting a causal seed begins the process of removing the stains from these five, allowing for them to function more purely. In this sense, implanting a causal seed acts as a circumstance for a foundational seed eventually to function fully.

Evolving factors include our bountiful stores of positive potential and deep awareness. With enlightenment, these transform, respectively, into our bodies with form (*rupakaya*) and bodies encompassing everything (*dharmakaya*), but are no longer present. Implanting causal seeds at an empowerment helps build up the foundational seeds of the two stores, and helps to remove certain obstacles preventing further development from happening.

An additional aspect of Buddha-nature makes the process of empowerment possible. This is the aspect of clear light mind that allows for its abiding and evolving factors to be affected by the enlightening influence of the Buddhas. Because of this aspect, the implanting of causal seeds at an empowerment affects the transformation of foundational seeds into Buddha-bodies. In the case of abiding factors, it affects them in the sense of stimulating the process of purification to occur. In the case of evolving factors, it stimulates the foundational seeds to grow.

APPLICATION TO KALACHAKRA EMPOWERMENT

The four subtle drops presented in Kalachakra are not aspects of Buddha-nature, nor are they foundational seeds. Rather, they are gateways to aspects of clear light mind that are included in Buddha-nature and which function as foundational seeds. The body, speech, mind and deep awareness drops are the gateways for the ability of clear light mind to give rise, respectively, to gross appearances, subtle appearances and sound, non-conceptual states and blissful awareness. When the winds of karma gather around and obscure these four drops, the mind, likewise obscured with confusion about reality, gives rise to the four most commonly deceptive experiences — the experiences of the gross appearances of being awake, of the subtle appearances and sounds of dreaming, of the non-conceptual state of deep dreamless sleep and of the bliss of orgasmic release. When all levels of fleeting obscuration are removed from the four subtle drops, the foundational seeds of clear light mind that allow for appearance-making and so forth give rise instead to the four bodies of a Buddha.

The four Buddha-bodies parallel and replace the four deceptive states. The appearances of *nirmanakaya*, a body of emanations, supplant the gross appearances of being awake. The subtle appearances and speech of *sambhogakaya*, a body of full use, replace the subtle appearances and sounds of dreams. The omniscient non-conceptual mind of *jnana-dharmakaya*, a body of deep awareness encompassing everything, replaces the blank non-conceptual mind of deep dreamless sleep. And the omniscient blissful awareness of *svabhavakaya*, a nature body, supplants the confusing bliss of orgasmic release. Kalachakra is unique in asserting that this nature body is the blissful awareness of a Buddha's omniscient mind.

Implanting causal seeds with Kalachakra empowerment begins to remove obscuration from the four subtle drops and acts as a circumstance for the foundational seeds that underlie the four to give rise to the immediate causes for the four Buddha-bodies during complete stage practice. When we attain enlightenment, we no longer have these four subtle drops. They dissolve into a rainbow along with the rest of our corporeal form and the foundational seeds that had functioned through them transform into the four Buddha-bodies. This is the mechanism, then, for purifying the four subtle drops in order to attain the four Buddha-bodies.

EXPERIENCING BLISSFUL AWARENESS OF VOIDNESS DURING EMPOWERMENT

Causal empowerment implants two seeds. One is a conscious experience, the other is a seed, trace or potential that this experience leaves on the mind-stream and which grows to maturity through cultivation with meditational practice. In anuttarayoga tantra, including Kalachakra, the conscious experience is always a blissful awareness of voidness. Such awareness is what actually purifies the mind-stream of confusion and obstacles, allowing for the attainment of all good qualities.

The Seventh Dalai Lama has explained that for most people, especially those with little meditational experience, it is difficult to generate a blissful awareness of voidness during an initiation. It is essential, however, to feel something constructive in order for the empowerment to occur. He therefore has recommended that we generate a feeling of happiness by whatever means we can and then direct that happy state of mind at whatever level of understanding of voidness we have. No matter how feeble a blissful awareness of voidness we generate, it is still a conscious experience that can act as a reference point for our subsequent practice. Without some active conscious experience, we are left without a trace of anything with which to work in meditation. If, however, we have such an experience during the empowerment and can easily recall it, we have an effective seed we can cultivate. Remembering the crowd, the ritual splendor, or our confusion when we got lost in the visualizations, hardly helps us make progress along the path to enlightenment.

For example, if, after tossing the flower in the mandala, we do not feel any particular joy at being crowned with a flower garland, we can recall any joyous moment we have had, such as the birth of a child or the return of a loved one. As for an accessible understanding of the voidness of inherent existence on which to focus in this state of mind, let me repeat the example I used during a series of talks delivered at the Kalachakra initiation conferred by His Holiness the present Dalai Lama in Rikon, Switzerland, in July 1985.

GENERATING AN UNDERSTANDING OF VOIDNESS

The weather was extremely hot, and someone had kindly provided me with a chilled can of club soda on the table in front of my seat. When we apprehend something, such as this can of soda, as existing with an inherent, findable identity, we believe it exists as what it is by virtue of some findable characteristic from its own side. We imagine, whether consciously or not, that there is something on the side of the soda that can be pointed to that gives it its concrete, lasting identity. We can think, "This can of soda is in front of my seat. It is mine, not yours. Don't touch it!" or, "This can is ice cold. I hate drinking anything cold. And look, it has a flip-top which I usually manage to cut my finger on. What a horrible can of soda!" In this way, we imagine the can of club soda sitting there, defiantly on the table, existing with a concrete, inherent identity as something very annoying from its own side, independently of the kind intentions of the person who brought it. Projecting, apprehending and then believing it to truly exist in the way our mind makes it appear, we become extremely upset and make ourselves miserable.

How does this can of club soda actually exist? On the deepest level, it exists devoid of being inherently nasty and disappointing. The paranoid vision of the can — that it is spitefully sitting there, trying to annoy us — is a total fantasy. It implies a fantasized and impossible way of existing which does not refer to anything real. A can of soda cannot have an intention, because it is cold, to upset our stomach. There is no such thing as an inherently annoying can of soda. If a can of soda were disappointing or annoying from its own side, it would have to be disappointing to everyone. There were many people listening to me that hot afternoon, I am sure, who would have loved to have had that soda and would not have considered it disappointing or annoying at all. Voidness, then, is a total absence of strange, impossible ways of existing that we fantasize and project onto persons, objects or situations.

It is more useful during the empowerment, however, to generate an understanding of the voidness of something more relevant to what is happening than a can of club soda. The reality of the situation of the empowerment, for instance, is not that there is some exotic event occurring on stage, and that we are completely separated and alienated from it in the audience, unable to follow what is happening. It is not like in a children's coloring book in which there are solid thick lines around the spiritual master up on the throne and ourselves down in the audience, rendering us totally unrelated entities existing on our own. Such a scene is a total fantasy and completely absent.

In fact, the situation during the empowerment is very open, and the laws of cause and effect are surely operating. The master is saying and doing various things, and we are experiencing something in response. Through this interchange, we are planting seeds that form the basis for future success in the practice. Even if we think merely of the absence of any solid thick lines around ourselves and our teacher, and focus on this in a happy state of mind — for instance, with the joy of relief that this is so — we gain empowerment for our understanding and insight to grow. Empowerment does not occur by magic, but arises dependently on our teacher's actions, our feelings in response, the implanting of causal seeds as a result of these two, our foundational seeds and the aspect of our clear light mind that allows for these seeds to be affected by an enlightening influence. Therefore, it is not necessary to have the most sophisticated experience of voidness and bliss at the initiation. However, we do need some experience on which to build.

THEORETICAL BASIS FOR THE SEVEN EMPOWERMENTS OF ENTERING LIKE A CHILD

The second day of the actual empowerment begins with the participants standing in the form of Vajravega and observers as simple Kalachakra in the black eastern entrance hall on the ground floor of the palace, as at the end of the previous day. If we are an observer, we remain in this hall for the rest of the empowerment, bearing witness to the events that follow. As a participant, we start the procedure by requesting the seven empowerments of entering like a child, and our teacher, Kalachakra, makes an offering into a fire to clear away anything inauspicious or detrimental to this. These seven empowerments are analogous to different stages of childhood and purify various aspects of body and mind. The analogy is fitting since, at the start of the preparation ceremony, we were born as the spiritual child of our teacher, Kalachakra. The water empowerment, the first of the seven, is analogous to our parents giving us our first bath; the crown empowerment, to their tying up our hair in a bun on the top of our head; the ear tassel — a ribbon that hangs from our ears — to their piercing our ears; the vajra and bell, to their making us smile and teaching us to say our first words; the tamed behavior, to their giving us our first pleasurable sensory objects to enjoy; the name, to their giving us a formal name — by Indian custom, at a ceremony approximately a year after birth; and the subsequent permission empowerment, to our parents teaching us to read.

The seven empowerments are conferred in four successive sets to purify the stains of the four subtle drops and plant seeds to attain vajra body, speech, mind and deep awareness. These are equivalent to the four Buddha-bodies, although the four higher and highest empowerments plant the actual causal seeds that ripen into these bodies. The first three sets consist of two empowerments each, while the last contains only one. Each set is conferred from the face of our teacher, Kalachakra, that corresponds to the color of the appropriate drop. This means that for each set we circumambulate to the side of the mandala corresponding in color to that face and receive an inner empowerment — as in the preparation ceremony — passing through the mouth of that face. We then sit in the entrance hall of that side of the palace in the form of the appropriate couple, the male figures of which are the same colors as the side in which we sit and are named Vajra Body, Vajra Speech, Vajra Mind and Vajra Deep Awareness, respectively. Thus, we receive the first two empowerments from the white body face in the north; the second two from the red speech face in the south; the next two from the black mind face in the east; and the last one from the yellow deep awareness face in the west. We pass from one side of the mandala to the next by walking clockwise through the same corridor as we did when offering prostration to the male Buddhas the day before. As a couple, we always embrace a partner who is the color of the opposite side of the palace from our immediate location — black goes with yellow, and white with red. These pairings symbolically harmonize the elements that normally destroy each other — wind blows away earth, while earthen walls block wind; water douses fire, while fire boils away water.

Each of these seven empowerments also purifies an aspect of our ordinary body or mind which is associated with the obscuration of the four drops. The first two empowerments purify the five elements and five aggregates, respectively. When the winds of karma gather at the body drop and we are involved with the atoms of our bodily elements and the aggregate factors of our experience, our clear light mind gives rise to the appearances of being awake. This prevents it from giving rise to a vajra body devoid of atoms. The second two empowerments purify, respectively, the ten energy-winds and right and left energy-channels. When the winds of karma gather at the speech drop and the ten energy-winds course through our right and left channels, we experience the appearances of dreams. This prevents these winds from entering the central channel, dissolving at the center of the six chakras, and reinforcing the vibration of our subtlest sound so that it becomes vajra speech.

The next two empowerments purify, respectively, the six cognitive sensors and their objects and the six functional parts of the body and their activities. When the winds of karma gather at the mind drop, temporarily withdrawing from cognitive and functional activities, we experience the appearances of deep dreamless sleep. This prevents them from withdrawing even further and dissolving at the center of the six chakras in the central energy-channel so that our clear light mind gives rise to vajra mind. The last of the seven empowerments of entering like a child purifies the deep awareness aggregate and consciousness element. When the winds of karma gather at the deep awareness drop, this aggregate and element give rise to the bliss of orgasmic release, while our clear light mind gives rise to the appearances of this peak experience. This prevents our realization of vajra deep awareness — the blissful awareness devoid of any such release or end.

Furthermore, each of these seven empowerments plants causal seeds to transform the specific factor purified — for example, the five bodily elements or aggregates — into Buddha-figures from the mandala. We need to understand clearly what this means in the context of Kalachakra. When our four subtle drops are stained with the winds of karma and our clear light mind is temporarily associated with confusion, this subtlest level of our mind gives rise to internal cycles of ordinary elements, aggregates and so forth, which further our suffering in samsara. When we cleanse our drops of these stains and replace confusion with blissful awareness of voidness, our clear light mind gives rise, instead, to alternative cycles of Buddha-figures to benefit others. This occurs because clear light mind continuously gives rise to appearances. This feature is one of the aspects of Buddha-nature.

This transformation begins when we receive the Kalachakra initiation. During causal empowerment, at the circumstance of feeling the physical sensation of being touched with a ritual implement — water from a vase, a crown and so forth — we gain a conscious experience of a blissful awareness of voidness, on whatever level we can manage it. This experience plants causal seeds to manifest, later through pathway and resultant empowerment, our clear light mind and to generate it as an unchanging blissful deep awareness of voidness. That future attainment activates clear light mind's appearance-making function, as a foundational seed, so that it gives rise to actual Buddha-figures rather than ordinary bodily elements, aggregates and so on. In this way, each of the seven empowerments plants seeds for being able to build up a vast amount of positive potential for this future attainment. In the initiation ritual our teacher, Kalachakra, explains that with each progressive empowerment we build up as much potential as bodhisattvas do as they progressively develop the *bhumi*, or levels of mind, after clear light realization of voidness.

THE COMMON STRUCTURE OF THE SEVEN EMPOWERMENTS

The procedure for each of these empowerments is complicated. The visualizations are extremely complex and difficult to execute unless we are well trained. The seven empowerments, however, share a common structure. Having an overview of this structure is helpful for being able to follow the initiation. Each empowerment involves a ritual implement, certain features of our body or mind, and a group of figures in the mandala. Let us use the example of the first of the seven, the water empowerment. It involves the water in a vase, our five bodily elements and the five female Buddhas.

First we withdraw our mind from making the water and our bodily elements appear in an ordinary fashion. This is done by focusing on their voidness — their total absence of impossible, fantasized ways of existing. We then generate an appearance of them in a pure form, as the five female Buddhas, each embracing a male partner. It is not so important to be able to visualize all the details. What is most important is to remove any confused, disturbing feelings we might have about how the water or our elements exist — such as the water being inherently foul-tasting due to chlorine, or our body being inherently too heavy, regardless of how much weight we lose. We generate the feeling, instead, that the water and our bodily elements are pure containers — as represented by the female Buddhas — for holding the ability to confer blissful awareness of voidness when they come in contact with each other. To enhance this feeling, our teacher, Kalachakra, dissolves deep awareness beings into the water and our elements as female Buddhas, as he did with ourselves as Vajravega during the preparation ceremony the day before.

At this point, there are three groups of five female Buddhas — the actual five in the mandala, the five that were the water of the vase and the five that were the elements of our body. First, the actual ones in the mandala come from their seats and give empowerment to the female Buddhas of the water of the vase. The latter then transform back into water, fully empowered to confer blissful awareness of voidness by the sensation of its touch. The five female Buddhas come once again from the mandala and touch the vase to the crown of our heads. We experience blissful awareness of voidness, while nectars flow from the vase, conferring empowerment to the five female Buddhas of our body. Our teacher, Kalachakra, then dabs water from a conch shell on five spots of our body and gives us a sip to drink. This acts as a circumstance for enhancing our blissful awareness of voidness even further. Finally, the female Buddhas in the mandala emanate a replica of themselves, which merges with the female Buddhas of our body, stabilizing our experience.

This basic structure repeats for all seven empowerments of entering like a child. Butön gives the same procedures as the Seventh Dalai Lama, except that he makes no mention of partners in conjunction with the female Buddhas of the water or our body. Kongtrül follows Butön on this point concerning the figures of the water, and does not mention at all the elements of our body transforming into female Buddhas at the start of the procedure. In his version, the female Buddhas of the water only have deep awareness beings dissolved into them, and there is no mention of their receiving empowerment or transforming back into the water of the vase. Specially invited empowering figures, with no mention of the female Buddhas from the mandala, touch the vase to our head and dab the five spots of our body. Only with the experience of blissful awareness of voidness is there mention of our elements transforming into the five female Buddhas, and there is no mention of their partners. Specially invited Buddhas and bodhisattvas, in the form of the five female Buddhas without partners — and without replicas emanated by the female Buddhas from the mandala — dissolve into the female Buddhas of our body. When we receive a Kalachakra initiation conferred according to either Butön or Kongtrül's text, we can either visualize only as much as the author explicitly describes, or fill in the details that are left unspoken.

If all these visualizations are too difficult to imagine, it is best to simply generate a happy state of mind and focus it on whatever understanding of voidness we have. If we feel frustrated at not being able to keep up with all the steps that are happening and we apprehend the whole process as being inherently too complicated and impossible to follow, we lose the opportunity to implant causal seeds for our future practice. Therefore, it is extremely important to focus on the essence of the empowerment process — gaining a conscious experience of blissful awareness of voidness, and feeling, with confidence, that we now have a reference point for further cultivation in future meditation. If we are attending as an interested observer, it is helpful to stay mindful of our foundational seeds and draw inspiration, from witnessing the ceremony, that future spiritual development is definitely possible. If we focus on how there is nothing magical or strange about initiations and the tantric path, and feel happy at that, we have already added a few bricks to this foundation.

FINAL APPENDED PROCEDURES

There are several additional steps appended to the last of the seven empowerments of entering like a child — the subsequent permission empowerment. This empowerment, although sharing the same name, is not the same as the subsequent permission ceremony that is sometimes appended as an additional day after the entire empowerment. Here, after the procedures common to the previous six empowerments, our teacher, Kalachakra, places a wheel of Dharma in front of our seat, a text in our lap and gives us a conch shell and bell to hold in our right and left hands respectively. We repeat a verse reaffirming our commitment to training with method and wisdom, the essence of the Dharma, in order to help others fully. We then transform from a yellow Vajra Deep Awareness with a black partner into a full blue Kalachakra with a yellow partner and receive the three main

Kalachakra mantras, repeating each three times. Neither Butön nor Kongtrül mentions this transformation. Finally we are given, one by one, eye medicine, a mirror, and a set of bow and arrows, which plant seeds for gaining, respectively, conceptual understanding of voidness, subsequent realization of everything to be like an illusion, and non-conceptual straightforward perception of voidness during total absorption.

The next step appended to the subsequent permission empowerment is the vajra master initiation. This should not be confused with the great vajra master empowerment, which is the final set of initiations conferred after the highest four empowerments when the Kalachakra initiation is given in its fullest form. The vajra master initiation confers close bonds for body, speech and mind. For this, the empowering implements are a vajra and bell. We and the vajra transform into a blue Vajrasattva, and the bell transforms into a blue Prajnaparamita. None have partners. The teacher, Kalachakra, dissolves deep awareness beings into all three of us. The five female Buddhas give empowerment to the Vajrasattva and Prajnaparamita which were the vajra and bell, and they transform back into these ritual implements. We are then given the vajra and bell to hold as the close bonds for our mind and speech, respectively. Keeping a vajra symbolizes closely bonding our mind to blissful deep awareness of voidness, while keeping a bell represents closely bonding our speech to always teaching this realization of voidness. Regarding our body, in the form of Vajrasattva, as the appearance to which blissful deep awareness of voidness naturally gives rise, we closely bond our body to this appearance. Experiencing blissful awareness of voidness while mindful of these three close bonds empowers us to actualize them in the future.

Butön has the bell transformed into a yellow Vishvamata — for whom blue Prajnaparamita is a common substitute, as we saw in the preparation ceremony — and makes no mention of our transformation into Vajrasattva until we receive the close bond for our body. At that point, we arise as a couple, embracing a Vishvamata, and not as a single figure. Kongtrül abbreviates the vajra master empowerment and does not mention any transformation of the vajra, bell or ourselves. Furthermore, he outlines receiving close bonds for only mind and speech, and not for body.

Of the initiations discussed so far, the vajra master empowerment is the one that specifically requires commitment to the tantric vows and closely bonding practices. Of the nineteen closely bonding practices common to all anuttarayoga systems, maintaining the close bonds of mind and body, established with this empowerment, constitute the first three of the four practices that create bonds with the family trait of Akshobhya — deep awareness of the sphere of reality. It is therefore fitting that the Kalachakra ritual includes the vajra master empowerment within the subsequent permission initiation to purify the deep awareness drop. Our teacher, Kalachakra, appropriately concludes this seventh empowerment of entering like a child by explaining the uncommon practices, unique to the Kalachakra system, that create close bonds with the six Buddha-families.

Finally, our teacher, Kalachakra explains that the entire set of seven initiations empowers us for generation stage practice, and then mentions, for future astrological reference, the exact time and date of the empowerment. Explaining the fourteen Kalachakra root tantric vows, he outlines the procedure for restoring them if we lose them completely. This method is to repeat 36,000 times the mantra of the principal male figure of the Buddha-family with which we have the closest link, as indicated by the flower tossed into the mandala on the day before. We then need to retake the seven empowerments of entering like a child. This can be done either at an initiation conferred by a tantric master, or, if we have completed a Kalachakra retreat during which we recite hundreds of thousands of mantras, at a self-initiation ceremony we conduct ourselves. We repeat three times our agreement to follow this procedure and then offer a mandala in thanksgiving to conclude the Kalachakra initiation.

CONCLUDING REMARKS

If we have received the Kalachakra empowerment from the Gelug tradition, as a practitioner we begin a daily program of six-session yoga to nurture the causal seeds implanted and to reinforce the purifications received. If we have received the empowerment from another tradition, we simply keep our vows and follow our closely bonding practices to accomplish the same. In either case, we give life to this ongoing process by repeatedly focusing each day and night on blissful awareness of voidness. This is most important, especially when we are feeling stressed or caught in the heat of a disturbing emotion. By returning to our clear light basis and then recomposing ourselves as a Kalachakra, we maintain a steady course in our life toward enlightenment and fully benefiting others.

If we attend a Kalachakra initiation as an observer, it is important not forget our experience. Although we have taken no formal commitment for daily practice, if we follow the example of the people of Shambhala who united in the Kalachakra mandala to form one caste, we receive lasting benefit. Thus it is extremely helpful to make a commitment to world peace and harmony through following purely the ethical teachings of the religion or creed to which we subscribe. With such a commitment, Kalachakra initiation has a profoundly positive effect on everyone.

CHAPTER TWELVE
Outline of the Initiation

The following outline is intended as an overview of the three days of the Kalachakra initiation. Those attending the ritual may find it helpful as a guide to the stages of the ceremony. Since most people find the diacritical marks on letters of Sanskrit seed-syllables of little significance during the initiation, they are omitted.

THE PREPARATION CEREMONY

A. SETTING THE MOTIVATION AND CONFERRING INNER EMPOWERMENT

1. We rinse our mouth, prostrate three times and offer a mandala.
2. Our teacher, Kalachakra, explains the proper motivation for receiving initiation.
3. Inner Empowerment. Rays of light from the heart of our fatherly teacher, Kalachakra, draw us into his mouth. Melting into a drop of bodhichitta and passing through his vajra-organ, we enter the lotus-womb of our mother, Vishvamata. There, we dissolve all ordinary appearances by focusing on voidness. While maintaining awareness of voidness, we arise first as a blue *HUM*, then as a blue vajra, and finally as a simple Kalachakra. We have one face, two arms, a blue body, right leg red and outstretched, left leg white and bent, and are without a partner. Light radiates from the heart of our teacher, Kalachakra, invoking all male and

female Buddhas. Entering through his mouth, melting in his heart with the fire of affection, and, in the form of drops of bodhichitta, passing through his vajra-organ into the lotus-womb of our mother, they empower us there. We radiate forth from the lotus-womb and take our place in the black eastern porch of the mandala palace.

B. REQUESTING VOWS AND CAUSING THE DISCIPLES TO TAKE FIRM HOLD OF TANTRA
1. We request safe direction, the trainings from the pledged state of aspiring bodhichitta, and bodhisattva vows by repeating a verse three times.
2. Our teacher, Kalachakra, explains about tantra in order to arouse our admiration for it.

C. TAKING VOWS, PROTECTING, AND BEING TRANSFORMED AND ELEVATED
1. We take safe direction and bodhisattva vows by repeating a verse three times.
2. We request and take the tantric vows. This is normally omitted and left to the next day.
3. Protecting the Disciples with Inseparable Method and Wisdom by Transforming Their Six Elements into the Nature of the Six Female Buddhas. We visualize that the water element of our body becomes a white syllable *U* standing upright on a white moon disc at our forehead; the wind element becomes a black *I* on a black Rahu disc at our heart; the space element becomes a green *A* on a green creative drop at the crown of our head; the earth element becomes a yellow *LI* on a yellow Kalagni disc at our navel; the fire element becomes a red *RI* on a red sun disc at our throat; and the consciousness element becomes a blue *AH* on a blue deep awareness disc at our pubic area.
4. Transformation and Elevation of the Disciples' Body, Speech and Mind. We visualize at our heart on a black Rahu disc a black *HUM* for mind, at our throat on a red sun disc a red *AH* for speech, and at our forehead on a white moon disc a white *OM* for body. Our teacher, Kalachakra, touches these three spots with the vajra in his hand, sprinkling drops of water from a conch shell. He makes offerings to us.

D. TOSSING THE TWIG OF A NEEM TREE AND GIVING SIPS OF WATER AND OTHER ITEMS

1. To determine the actual attainments we can most readily achieve, we toss the twig of a neem tree onto a tray with a mandala drawn in it. We do this by holding the twig vertically in both hands directly above the tray and letting it fall, while reciting a mantra.
2. We receive a handful of water. First rinsing our mouth with a little of it, we spit that out and drink the rest in three sips. This purifies the stains of our body, speech and mind.
3. We receive two pieces of kusha grass, one long and one short. We place them in our lap.
4. We receive a red protection string, which we tie around the upper part of either our left or right arm. We wear this string until either Maitreya Buddha comes, or we develop pure love.

E. ARRANGING THE SIX BUDDHA-FAMILIES AND INVOKING VAJRASATTVA

1. We visualize the seed-syllables of the six male Buddhas at six places on our body: at our forehead a white *OM*, at our throat a red *AH*, at our heart a black *HUM*, at our navel a yellow *HOH*, at the crown of our head a green *HAM* and at our pubic region a blue *KSHAH*. The six Buddhas from the mandala emanate replicas of themselves, which enter and dissolve into the six syllables.
2. We repeat a long mantra for invoking Vajrasattva to transform and elevate our body, speech and mind.

F. ENHANCING THE DISCIPLES' HAPPINESS BY EXPLAINING THE DHARMA, AND INSTRUCTING THEM TO EXAMINE THEIR DREAMS

1. Our teacher, Kalachakra, enhances our happiness by explaining how rare the opportunity is to meet with the tantra teachings.
2. He bestows the six-syllable mantra, *OM AH HUM HO HAM KSHAH*, which we repeat after him. (In Tibetan "ham kshah" is pronounced "hankya.") He instructs us to recite this mantra before retiring this evening and to place the long reed of kusha grass under our mattress, parallel to our body, with the tips pointing toward our head, and the short reed under our pillow, perpendicular to the long one, and with the tips pointing away from our face as we lie on our right side. He recommends we sleep in this

position with our head facing the mandala. Even if our head is not oriented in the proper direction, we imagine and feel that it is. He tells us to observe and remember the dreams we have at the first break of dawn, just as the sky begins to turn light.

THE FIRST DAY OF THE ACTUAL EMPOWERMENT

I. ENTERING BLINDFOLDED, REMAINING OUTSIDE THE CURTAIN

1. We rinse our mouth with water and prostrate three times. Our teacher, Kalachakra, explains not to be proud if we have had an auspicious dream or depressed if we have had an ominous one. All dreams are void of inherent existence. He offers a torma to dispel interference. We offer a mandala.

2. To generate happiness at the opportunity to achieve the highest actual attainment of enlightenment, we repeat a long mantra twice in Sanskrit and once in Tibetan.

3. We request safe direction, the trainings from the pledged state of aspiring bodhichitta, and bodhisattva vows by repeating a verse three times.

4. The main disciples receive a ritual lower garment, upper garment and crown protrusion. We all receive red blindfold ribbons, which we drape across our forehead, and a flower, which we hold in our lap.

5. We toss the twig from a neem tree and take three sips of water for purification, as on the day before.

6. We transform into a simple Kalachakra, with one face and two arms, holding vajra and bell, with a blue body, right leg red and outstretched, left leg white and bent, and embracing a blue Vishvamata, with one face and two arms, holding a cleaver and skullcup. We visualize at our heart on a black Rahu disc a black *HUM*, at our throat on a red sun disc a red *AH*, and at our forehead on a white moon disc a white *OM*. Light from these three syllables fills our body, transforming it into clear light.

7. Our teacher, Kalachakra, asks us our family trait, hinayana or mahayana, and what we admire. We answer that we are fortunate ones, with a mahayana Buddha-nature, and we seek the greatly blissful awareness of enlightenment.

8. Repeating a plaintive verse declaring our need for safe direction, we take refuge and bodhisattva vows by repeating another verse three times.

9. We request tantric vows, by repeating a verse, and then take them by repeating another verse three times.

10. Our teacher, Kalachakra, explains the twenty-five modes of tamed behavior. We repeat three times a verse promising to uphold them.

11. The Yoga Encompassing Everything. Dedicating our heart to attaining enlightenment in order to benefit everyone, we generate conventional bodhichitta, visualizing it in the form of a white moon disc lying flat at our heart. We then generate deepest bodhichitta, a mind focused on voidness. We visualize this as an upright white vajra standing on the moon disc at our heart. We repeat a mantra, affirming that we shall always keep these attitudes in our heart and mind. Our teacher, Kalachakra, emanates a replica of the two from a similar moon disc and vajra at his heart, which dissolves into the moon and vajra at our heart. Holding a flower and vajra at our heart, he recites a mantra, stabilizing these attitudes.

12. Our teacher, Kalachakra, places his vajra on our head and reminds us to maintain confidentiality.

II. ENTERING BLINDFOLDED INTO THE MANDALA PALACE
A. ENTERING, CIRCUMAMBULATING AND PROSTRATING
1. With the curtain now drawn aside, we enter the mandala palace through the black eastern doorway. Blindfolded, we are led by blue Karmavajra, the emanated assistant of our teacher, Kalachakra. Karmavajra holds out in his right hand, which contains a vajra. We take hold of it with our left hand and circumambulate the ground floor clockwise three times, in the corridor between the wall and raised platform, while repeating a mantra.
2. In the black eastern entrance hall, we transform into a green Akshobhya and prostrate to the main figure three times while repeating a mantra. A replica of Akshobhya from the mandala dissolves into us.
3. Remaining in the black eastern entrance hall, we transform into a black Amoghasiddhi and prostrate to him three times while

repeating a mantra. A replica of Amoghasiddhi from the mandala dissolves into us.

4. Circumambulating clockwise to the red southern entrance hall, we transform into a red Ratnasambhava and prostrate to him three times while repeating a mantra. A replica of Ratnasambhava from the mandala dissolves into us.

5. Circumambulating clockwise to the white northern entrance hall, we transform into a white Amitabha and prostrate to him three times while repeating a mantra. A replica of Amitabha from the mandala dissolves into us.

6. Circumambulating clockwise to the yellow western doorway, we transform into a yellow Vairochana and prostrate to him three times while repeating a mantra. A replica of Vairochana from the mandala dissolves into us.

7. Circumambulating clockwise to the black eastern doorway while remaining as a yellow Vairochana, we prostrate to our teacher, Kalachakra, three times while repeating a mantra.

B. SWEARING OF OATHS

1. Placing his vajra on our head, our teacher, Kalachakra, explains the benefits of keeping confidentiality.

2. Keeping his vajra on our head, he explains the physical drawbacks of not keeping it.

3. Placing his vajra at our heart, he explains the mental drawbacks of not keeping it.

4. Explaining both the advantages of keeping confidentiality and the disadvantages of breaking it, he gives us a sip of vajra oath-swearing water from a conch shell.

5. Our teacher, Kalachakra, takes our hand and explains the importance of never disparaging our vajra master.

C. INVOKING DEEP AWARENESS BEINGS TO DESCEND AND RECITING WORDS OF TRUTH

1. We repeat three times a verse of request. We dissolve all appearances by focusing on voidness. While maintaining awareness of voidness, we arise as a blue *HUM* and transform into a full Vajravega, fierce and forceful, with a blue body, four faces, twenty-six arms and two legs. At our navel, from *LAM* comes a square yellow earth mandala marked with a wheel, and on it, on a yellow Kalagni disc is a yellow *HOH*, standing upright. At our heart, from *YAM* comes a black bow-shaped wind

mandala marked with two banners, and on it, on a black Rahu disc is an upright black *HUM*. At our throat, from *RAM* comes a triangular red fire mandala marked with a jewel, and on it, on a red sun disc is an upright red *AH*. At our forehead, from *VAM* comes a white round water mandala marked with a vase, and on it, on a white moon disc is an upright white *OM*. Light radiates from these four syllables and from the heart of our teacher, Kalachakra, and brings back four Buddha-figures — white Vajra Body, red Vajra Speech, black Vajra Mind and yellow Vajra Deep Awareness — who dissolve into these four syllables.

2. Below our feet, from *YAM* comes a black bow-shaped wind mandala marked with *YAM*. On it, from *RAM* comes a red triangular fire mandala marked with *RAM*. On it, on each of the two soles of our feet is a red *JHAI* radiating light. Light from the heart of our teacher, Kalachakra, strikes the wind mandala, making it turbulent, which causes the fire mandala to blaze. Light from the two syllables *JHAI* radiates through the pores of the soles of our feet, stimulating the syllables on the four planet discs, which emit light that fills our entire body. At the same time, light radiates from the heart of our teacher, Kalachakra, and brings back all the Buddhas in the form of Kalachakras and Vajravegas, who fill all of space and rain down upon us, dissolving into our body.

3. Reciting a mantra, our teacher, Kalachakra, tosses flower petals on our head.

4. We safeguard and stabilize the deep awareness beings' descent by sealing our six chakras with the seed-syllables of the six Buddha-family traits of method and wisdom. We visualize at our forehead a white *OM*, at our heart a black *HUM*, at the crown of our head a green *HAM*, at our navel a yellow *HOH*, at our throat a red *AH* and at our pubic region a blue *KSHAH*.

5. For a sign for our future attainment, we remove our blindfold for a moment, look up and observe the color we first see. We put our blindfolds back on.

6. Karmavajra, the emanated assistant of our teacher, Kalachakra, leads us in circumambulating the mandala clockwise three times.

7. Our teacher, Kalachakra, in the form of Karmavajra, stands at the eastern doorway of the mandala palace and recites words of truth, requesting that his disciples may be shown the Buddha-family with which they have the strongest connection.

III. ENTERING AS SOMEONE WHO CAN SEE THE MANDALA

1. Still in the form of a Vajravega, we offer to the mandala the flower we were given earlier. We hold the flower with both hands, directly over a tray which has a mandala drawn on it and is held on top of a vase. We let the flower fall while reciting a mantra. In accordance with the direction in which the flower lands, we learn the Buddha-family trait with which we have the closest affinity and receive the confidential name of that Buddha-family. We are given back the flower, which we place on the top of our head, while repeating a mantra. From the touch of the flower on the top of our head, we experience blissful awareness of voidness.

2. We remove our blindfold and see the mandala clearly. Our teacher, Kalachakra, describes the mandala and all the figures in it.

3. With joy at seeing the mandala, we recite a verse indicating our close bond.

THE SECOND DAY OF THE ACTUAL EMPOWERMENT

IV. GIVING THE EMPOWERMENTS TO THOSE WHO HAVE ENTERED

1. Still in the form of Vajravega, we request the seven empowerments of entering like a child by repeating a verse three times.

2. Our teacher, Kalachakra, makes offerings into a fire to purify anything inauspicious, and then makes other offerings.

A. WATER EMPOWERMENT

1. Led by an emanation of our teacher, Kalachakra, we circumambulate clockwise to the white northern entrance hall where we stand facing the white body face of our teacher, Kalachakra.

2. We offer a mandala requesting the water empowerment to purify our five bodily elements, and repeat three times a mantra of request.

3. Inner Empowerment. Rays of light from the heart of our teacher, Kalachakra, draw us into his mouth. Melting into a drop of bodhichitta and passing through his vajra-organ, we enter the lotus-womb of Vishvamata. There, we dissolve all ordinary appearances by focusing on voidness. While maintaining awareness of voidness, we arise first as a white *OM*, then a white lotus, and finally as a white Vajra Body, sitting crosslegged, with three faces and six arms, embracing a red Pandaravasin, also with three faces and six arms. Light radiating from

the heart of our teacher, Kalachakra, returns with deep awareness beings who merge with us as Vajra Body. Light radiates once more from his heart, invoking all male and female Buddhas. Our teacher, Kalachakra, makes offerings to them and requests that they empower his disciples. Happily agreeing, they enter into union and melt into the form of drops of bodhichitta. Entering through the crown of his head, descending through the center of his body and passing through his vajra-organ into the lotus-womb of Vishvamata, they empower us there. We radiate forth from the lotus-womb and return to the white northern entrance hall, where we take our seat.

4. Our teacher, Kalachakra, clears away interference and purifies into voidness our five bodily elements and the water of a vase. Within a state of voidness, our five elements and the water of the vase are generated as the five female Buddhas, sitting cross-legged and embracing the five male Buddhas, with all figures having three faces and six arms. Within our body, the five female Buddhas are located at our crown, forehead, throat, heart and navel chakras. On the forehead of each figure is a white *OM*, on the throat a red *AH*, at the heart a black *HUM* and at the navel a yellow *HOH*.

5. Light radiates from the heart of our teacher, Kalachakra, and returns with deep awareness beings who merge with the female Buddhas of the vase and our elements. The female Buddhas in the mandala empower the female Buddhas of the vase, and each receives as a crowning ornament the seal of the principal male figure of her Buddha-family. Our teacher, Kalachakra, makes offerings to the female Buddhas of the vase. They melt into drops of bodhichitta and transform back into the water of the vase.

6. Light radiates once more from the heart of our teacher, Kalachakra, invoking male and female Buddha and bodhisattva empowering figures. He makes offerings to them and requests them to empower his disciples. They agree. Some recite auspicious verses, others toss flowers, fierce ones chase away interference. Our teacher, Kalachakra, recites the auspicious verses, while his attendant, Karmavajra, holds up the vase. The female Buddhas in the mandala confer the actual water empowerment with white vases of bodhichitta, pouring some on the top of our head.

7. Our teacher, Kalachakra, reciting a verse and a mantra, dabs water from the conch shell on five spots on our body: the top of our head, our right and left shoulder and right and left hip. He then sprinkles some water to wash us and gives us a sip to drink. By being sprinkled and washed, we are purified of sufferings and stains; by drinking, we experience greatly blissful awareness of voidness. Our five bodily elements are now fully empowered as the five female Buddhas.

8. Light radiates from the five female Buddhas in our body and brings back from the mandala replicas of their counterparts there. They, as well as the other empowering figures, dissolve into the female Buddhas in our body. Our teacher, Kalachakra, makes an offering to us.

9. Our teacher, Kalachakra, explains that the water empowerment is analogous to washing an infant immediately after its birth. It washes away the stains of the five bodily elements and plants seeds on our mind-stream for realizing the five female Buddhas and the actual attainments that depend on them. It grants the ability to achieve positive potential equivalent to someone with a first bodhisattva level of mind.

B. CROWN EMPOWERMENT

1. We offer a mandala requesting the crown empowerment to purify the five aggregate factors of our experience, and repeat three times a mantra of request.

2. Our teacher, Kalachakra, clears away interference and purifies into voidness our five aggregates and a crown. Within a state of voidness, our five aggregates and the crown are generated as the five male Buddhas, sitting cross-legged and embracing the five female Buddhas, with all figures having three faces and six arms. Within our body, the five male Buddhas are located at our crown, forehead, throat, heart and navel chakras. On the forehead of each figure is a white *OM*, on the throat a red *AH*, at the heart a black *HUM* and at the navel a yellow *HOH*.

3. Light radiates from the heart of our teacher, Kalachakra, and returns with deep awareness beings who merge with the male Buddhas of the crown and our aggregates. The male Buddhas in the mandala empower the male Buddhas of the crown, and each receives as a crowning ornament the seal of the principal male figure of his Buddha-family. Our teacher, Kalachakra,

makes offerings to the male Buddhas of the crown. They melt into drops of bodhichitta and transform back into the crown.

4. Light radiates once more from the heart of our teacher, Kalachakra, invoking male and female Buddha and bodhisattva empowering figures. He makes offerings to them and requests them to empower his disciples. They agree. Some recite auspicious verses, others toss flowers, fierce ones chase away interference. Our teacher, Kalachakra, recites the auspicious verses, while his attendant, Karmavajra, holds up the crown. The male Buddhas in the mandala confer the actual crown empowerment by touching the crown to the five spots on our body and then placing it on our head to wear. At its touch, we experience greatly blissful awareness of voidness. Our teacher, Kalachakra, reciting a verse and a mantra, confers a concluding water empowerment by dabbing and sprinkling water from the conch shell and giving us a sip to drink, as before. Our five aggregates are now fully empowered as the five male Buddhas.

5. Light radiates from the five male Buddhas in our body and brings back from the mandala replicas of their counterparts there. They, as well as the other empowering figures, dissolve into the male Buddhas in our body. Our teacher, Kalachakra, makes an offering to us.

6. Our teacher, Kalachakra, explains that the crown empowerment is analogous to piling a baby's hair into a bun on top of its head. It washes away the stains of the five aggregates and plants seeds on our mind-stream for realizing the five male Buddhas and the actual attainments that depend on them. It grants the ability to achieve positive potential equivalent to someone with a second bodhisattva level of mind. He further explains that the two empowerments received facing the white body face purify the stains of the body drop and plant seeds for attaining vajra body.

C. EAR TASSEL EMPOWERMENT

1. Led by an emanation of our teacher, Kalachakra, we circumambulate clockwise to the red southern entrance hall where we sit, facing the red speech face of our teacher, Kalachakra.

2. We offer a mandala requesting the ear tassel empowerment to purify our ten energy-winds, and repeat three times a mantra of request.

3. Inner Empowerment. Rays of light from the heart of our teacher, Kalachakra, draw us into his mouth. Melting into a drop of bodhichitta and passing through his vajra-organ, we enter the lotus-womb of Vishvamata. There, we dissolve all ordinary appearances by focusing on voidness. While maintaining awareness of voidness, we arise first as a red *AH*, then a red jewel, and finally as a red Vajra Speech, sitting cross-legged, with three faces and six arms, embracing a white Mamaki, also with three faces and six arms. Light radiates from the heart of our teacher, Kalachakra, and returns with deep awareness beings who merge with us as Vajra Speech. Light radiates once more from his heart, invoking all male and female Buddhas. Our teacher, Kalachakra, makes offerings to them and requests they empower his disciples. Happily agreeing, they enter into union and melt into the form of drops of bodhichitta. Entering through the crown of his head, descending through the center of his body and passing through his vajra-organ into the lotus-womb of Vishvamata, they empower us there. We radiate forth from the lotus-womb and return to the red southern entrance hall, where we take our seat.

4. Our teacher, Kalachakra, clears away interference and purifies into voidness our ten energy-winds and an ear tassel. Within a state of voidness, our ten energy-winds and the ear tassel are generated as the ten powerful ladies (*shaktis*) who are standing, with each having four faces and eight arms. Within our body, the ten are located on the energy-channels that radiate from our heart chakra. On the forehead of each is a white *OM*, on the throat a red *AH*, at the heart a black *HUM* and at the navel a yellow *HOH*.

5. Light radiates from the heart of our teacher, Kalachakra, and returns with deep awareness beings who merge with the powerful ladies of the ear tassel and our energy-winds. The powerful ladies in the mandala empower the powerful ladies of the ear tassel, and each receives as a crowning ornament the seal of the principal male figure of her Buddha-family. Our teacher, Kalachakra, makes offerings to the powerful ladies of the ear tassel. They melt into drops of bodhichitta and transform back into the ear tassel.

6. Light radiates once more from the heart of our teacher, Kalachakra, invoking male and female Buddha and bodhisattva empowering figures. He makes offerings to them and requests them to empower his disciples. They agree. Some recite auspicious verses, others toss flowers, fierce ones chase away interference. Our teacher, Kalachakra, recites the auspicious verses, while his attendant, Karmavajra, holds up the ear tassel. The powerful ladies in the mandala confer the actual ear tassel empowerment by touching the ear tassel to the five spots on our body and then draping a pair over our ears. At its touch, we experience greatly blissful awareness of voidness. Our teacher, Kalachakra, reciting a verse and a mantra, confers a concluding water empowerment by dabbing and sprinkling water from the conch shell and giving us a sip to drink, as before. Our ten energy-winds are now fully empowered as the ten powerful ladies.

7. Light radiates from the ten powerful ladies in our body and brings back from the mandala replicas of their counterparts there. They, as well as the other empowering figures, dissolve into the powerful ladies in our body. Our teacher, Kalachakra, makes an offering to us.

8. Our teacher, Kalachakra, explains that the ear tassel empowerment is analogous to piercing a baby's ears and giving it earrings to wear. It washes away the stains of the ten energy-winds and plants seeds on our mind-stream for realizing the ten powerful ladies and the actual attainments that depend on them. It grants the ability to achieve positive potential equivalent to someone with a third bodhisattva level of mind.

D. VAJRA AND BELL EMPOWERMENT

1. We offer a mandala requesting the vajra and bell empowerment to purify our right and left energy-channels, and repeat three times a mantra of request.

2. Our teacher, Kalachakra, clears away interference and purifies into voidness our right and left energy-channels and a vajra and bell. Within a state of voidness, our right channel and the vajra are generated as a blue Kalachakra, standing and embracing a yellow Vishvamata, while our left channel and the bell as a yellow Vishvamata, standing and embracing a blue

Kalachakra. Each of them has one face and two arms. Within our body, Kalachakra and Vishvamata are located at our right and left channels at our heart chakra. On the forehead of each figure is a white *OM*, on the throat a red *AH*, at the heart a black *HUM* and at the navel a yellow *HOH*.

3. Light radiates from the heart of our teacher, Kalachakra, and returns with deep awareness beings who merge with the Kalachakra and Vishvamata of the vajra and bell and our right and left channels. The Kalachakra and Vishvamata in the mandala empower the Kalachakra and Vishvamata of the vajra and bell, and each receives as a crowning ornament the seal of the principal male figure of his or her Buddha-family. Our teacher, Kalachakra, makes offerings to the Kalachakra and Vishvamata of the vajra and bell. They melt into drops of bodhichitta and transform back into the vajra and bell.

4. Light radiates once more from the heart of our teacher, Kalachakra, invoking male and female Buddha and bodhisattva empowering figures. He makes offerings to them and requests them to empower his disciples. They agree. Some recite auspicious verses, others toss flowers, fierce ones chase away interference. Our teacher, Kalachakra, recites the auspicious verses, while his attendant, Karmavajra, holds up the vajra and bell. The Vishvamata and Kalachakra couple in the mandala confer the actual vajra and bell empowerment by touching the vajra and bell to the five spots on our body and then giving them to us to hold in our crossed hands. At their touch, we experience greatly blissful awareness of voidness. Our teacher, Kalachakra, reciting a verse and a mantra, confers a concluding water empowerment by dabbing and sprinkling water from the conch shell and giving us a sip to drink, as before. Our right and left energy-channels are now fully empowered as Kalachakra and Vishvamata.

5. Light radiates from the Kalachakra and Vishvamata in our body and brings back from the mandala replicas of their counterparts there. They, as well as the other empowering figures, dissolve into the Kalachakra and Vishvamata in our body. Our teacher, Kalachakra, makes an offering to us.

6. Our teacher, Kalachakra, explains that the vajra and bell empowerment is analogous to making a baby smile and teaching it to speak its first words. It washes away the stains of the five

aggregates and confers the ability to stop our energy-winds from coursing through our right and left channels so that they enter, abide and dissolve in the central channel. It plants seeds for our mind to become unchanging blissful awareness, our speech to be endowed with all positive aspects and for us to gain the actual attainments that depend on Kalachakra and Vishvamata. It grants the ability to achieve positive potential equivalent to someone with a fourth bodhisattva level of mind. He further explains that the two empowerments received facing the red speech face purify the stains of the speech drop and plant seeds for attaining vajra speech.

E. TAMED BEHAVIOR EMPOWERMENT
  1. Led by an emanation of our teacher, Kalachakra, we circumambulate clockwise to the black eastern entrance hall where we sit, facing the black mind face of our teacher, Kalachakra.
  2. We offer a mandala requesting the tamed behavior empowerment to purify our six cognitive sensors and their objects, and repeat three times a mantra of request.
  3. Inner Empowerment. Rays of light from the heart of our teacher, Kalachakra, draw us into his mouth. Melting into a drop of bodhichitta and passing through his vajra-organ, we enter the lotus-womb of Vishvamata. There, we dissolve all ordinary appearances by focusing on voidness. While maintaining awareness of voidness, we arise first as a black *HUM*, then a black vajra, and finally as a black Vajra Mind, sitting cross-legged, with three faces and six arms, embracing a yellow Lochana, also with three faces and six arms. Light radiates from the heart of our teacher, Kalachakra, and returns with deep awareness beings who merge with us as Vajra Mind. Light radiates once more from his heart, invoking all male and female Buddhas. Our teacher, Kalachakra, makes offerings to them and requests they empower his disciples. Happily agreeing, they enter into union and melt into the form of drops of bodhichitta. Entering through the crown of his head, descending through the center of his body and passing through his vajra-organ into the lotus-womb of Vishvamata, they empower us there. We radiate forth from the lotus-womb and return to the black eastern entrance hall, where we take our seat.
  4. Our teacher, Kalachakra, clears away interference and purifies into voidness our six cognitive sensors and their six objects as

well as a thumb ring. Within a state of voidness, our six cognitive sensors and their six objects as well as the thumb ring are generated as the six male and six female bodhisattvas, sitting cross-legged and embracing six female and six male bodhisattvas respectively, with all figures having three faces and six arms. Within our body, the twelve are located, two each, at our ears, nose, eyes, tongue, the joints of our arms and legs, and our heart. On the forehead of each figure is a white *OM*, on the throat a red *AH*, at the heart a black *HUM* and at the navel a yellow *HOH*.

5. Light radiates from the heart of our teacher, Kalachakra, and returns with deep awareness beings who merge with the male and female bodhisattvas of the thumb ring and our cognitive sensors and their objects. The male and female bodhisattvas in the mandala empower the male and female bodhisattvas of the thumb ring, and each receives as a crowning ornament the seal of the principal male figure of his or her Buddha-family. Our teacher, Kalachakra, makes offerings to the male and female bodhisattvas of the thumb ring. They melt into drops of bodhichitta and transform back into the thumb ring.

6. Light radiates once more from the heart of our teacher, Kalachakra, invoking male and female Buddha and bodhisattva empowering figures. He makes offerings to them and requests them to empower his disciples. They agree. Some recite auspicious verses, others toss flowers, fierce ones chase away interference. Our teacher, Kalachakra, recites the auspicious verses, while his attendant, Karmavajra, holds up the thumb ring. The male and female bodhisattvas in the mandala confer the actual tamed behavior empowerment by touching the thumb ring to the five spots on our body and then putting it on our right thumb. At its touch, we experience greatly blissful awareness of voidness. Our teacher, Kalachakra, reciting a verse and a mantra, confers a concluding water empowerment by dabbing and sprinkling water from the conch shell and giving us a sip to drink, as before. Our six cognitive sensors and their six objects are now fully empowered as the six male and six female bodhisattvas.

7. Light radiates from the six male and six female bodhisattvas in our body and brings back from the mandala replicas of their counterparts there. They, as well as the other empowering

figures, dissolve into the male and female bodhisattvas in our body. Our teacher, Kalachakra, makes an offering to us.

8. Our teacher, Kalachakra, explains that the tamed behavior empowerment is analogous to giving a baby its first pleasurable sensory objects to enjoy. It washes away the stains of the six cognitive sensors and their six objects, and plants seeds on our mind-stream for realizing the six male and six female bodhisattvas and the actual attainments that depend on them. It grants the ability to achieve positive potential equivalent to someone with a fifth bodhisattva level of mind.

F. NAME EMPOWERMENT

1. We offer a mandala requesting the name empowerment to purify the six functional parts of our body and their six functional activities, and repeat three times a mantra of request.

2. Our teacher, Kalachakra, clears away interference and purifies into voidness our six functional bodily parts and their six activities as well as a bracelet. Within a state of voidness, our six functional parts and their six activities as well as the bracelet are generated as the six male and six female fierce figures, standing and embracing six female and six male fierce figures respectively, with all figures having three faces and six arms. Within our body, the twelve are located, two each, at the end of our urinary tract, our mouth, hands, feet, anus, and the bottom end of our central energy-channel. On the forehead of each figure is a white *OM,* on the throat a red *AH,* at the heart a black *HUM* and at the navel a yellow *HOH.*

3. Light radiates from the heart of our teacher, Kalachakra, and returns with deep awareness beings who merge with the male and female fierce figures of the bracelet and our functional parts and their activities. The male and female fierce figures in the mandala empower the male and female fierce figures of the bracelet, and each receives as a crowning ornament the seal of the principal male figure of his or her Buddha-family. Our teacher, Kalachakra, makes offerings to the male and female fierce figures of the bracelet. They melt into drops of bodhichitta and transform back into the bracelet.

4. Light· radiates once more from the heart of our teacher, Kalachakra, invoking male and female Buddha and bodhisattva empowering figures. He makes offerings to them and requests them to empower his disciples. They agree. Some recite

auspicious verses, others toss flowers, fierce ones chase away interference. Our teacher, Kalachakra, recites the auspicious verses, while his attendant, Karmavajra, holds up the bracelet. The male and female fierce figures in the mandala confer the actual tamed behavior empowerment by touching the bracelet to the five spots on our body and then putting one on each of our wrists. At their touch, we experience greatly blissful awareness of voidness. Our teacher, Kalachakra, reciting a verse and a mantra, confers a concluding water empowerment by dabbing and sprinkling water from the conch shell and giving us a sip to drink, as before.

5. Our teacher, Kalachakra, stands on his throne, dons a yellow monks' shawl and, in the manner of Shakyamuni Buddha, gathers the corners of the shawl in his left hand at his heart, holds his right hand in the fearless gesture and prophesies the form in which we shall become Buddhas. He makes the prophesy by reciting the confidential name conferred on us earlier when we offered a flower to the mandala, determining the Buddha-family trait with which we have the closest affinity. By means of the name empowerment conferred with this prophesy, the six functional parts of our body and their six functional activities are now fully empowered as the six male and six female fierce figures.

6. Light radiates from the six male and six female fierce figures in our body and brings back from the mandala replicas of their counterparts there. They, as well as the other empowering figures, dissolve into the male and female fierce figures in our body. Our teacher, Kalachakra, makes an offering to us.

7. Our teacher, Kalachakra, explains that the name empowerment is analogous to giving a child its name with a formal ceremony around its first birthday. It washes away the stains of the six functional parts of our body and their six activities. It confers the ability to overcome the four demonic forces (*mara*) with the four immeasurable attitudes and plants seeds on our mindstream for realizing the six male and six female fierce figures and the actual attainments that depend on them. It grants the ability to achieve positive potential equivalent to someone with a sixth bodhisattva level of mind. He further explains that the

two empowerments received facing the black mind face purify the stains of the mind drop and plant seeds for attaining vajra mind.

G. SUBSEQUENT PERMISSION EMPOWERMENT AND APPENDED PROCEDURES

1. Led by an emanation of our teacher, Kalachakra, we circumambulate clockwise to the yellow western entrance hall where we sit, facing the yellow deep awareness face of our teacher, Kalachakra.

2. We offer a mandala requesting the subsequent permission empowerment to purify our deep awareness aggregate and consciousness element, and repeat three times a mantra of request. This aggregate and element refer to our primordial clear light mind.

3. Inner Empowerment. Rays of light from the heart of our teacher, Kalachakra, draw us into his mouth. Melting into a drop of bodhichitta and passing through his vajra-organ, we enter the lotus-womb of Vishvamata. There, we dissolve all ordinary appearances by focusing on voidness. While maintaining awareness of voidness, we arise first as a yellow *HO*, then a yellow wheel and finally as a yellow Vajra Deep Awareness, sitting cross-legged, with three faces and six arms, embracing a black Tara, also with three faces and six arms. Light radiates from the heart of our teacher, Kalachakra, and returns with deep awareness beings who merge with us as Vajra Deep Awareness. Light radiates once more from his heart, invoking all male and female Buddhas. Our teacher, Kalachakra, makes offerings to them and requests they empower his disciples. Happily agreeing, they enter into union and melt into the form of drops of bodhichitta. Entering through the crown of his head, descending through the center of his body and passing through his vajra-organ into the lotus-womb of Vishvamata, they empower us there. We radiate forth from the lotus-womb and return to the yellow western entrance hall, where we take our seat.

4. Our teacher, Kalachakra, clears away interference and purifies into voidness our deep awareness aggregate and consciousness element and a set of insignia of the five Buddha-family traits. Within a state of voidness, our deep awareness aggregate

and consciousness element and the insignia are generated as a blue Vajrasattva and a blue Prajnaparamita, sitting cross-legged and embracing a green Vajradhatu Ishvari and a green Akshobhya, respectively, with all figures having three faces and six arms. Within our body, Vajrasattva and Prajnaparamita are located at our heart. On the forehead of each figure is a white *OM*, on the throat a red *AH*, at the heart a black *HUM* and at the navel a yellow *HOH*.

5. Light radiates from the heart of our teacher, Kalachakra, and returns with deep awareness beings who merge with the Vajrasattva and Prajnaparamita of the insignia and our deep awareness aggregate and consciousness element. The Vajrasattva and Prajnaparamita in the mandala empower the Vajrasattva and Prajnaparamita of the insignia, and each receives as a crowning ornament the seal of the principal male figure of his or her Buddha-family. Our teacher, Kalachakra, makes offerings to the Vajrasattva and Prajnaparamita of the insignia. They melt into drops of bodhichitta and transform back into the insignia.

6. Light radiates once more from the heart of our teacher, Kalachakra, invoking male and female Buddha and bodhisattva empowering figures. He makes offerings to them and requests them to empower his disciples. They agree. Some recite auspicious verses, others toss flowers, fierce ones chase away interference. Our teacher, Kalachakra, recites the auspicious verses, while his attendant, Karmavajra, holds up the insignia. The Vajrasattva and Prajnaparamita in the mandala confer the actual subsequent permission empowerment by touching the insignia to the five spots on our body and then giving the insignia for us to hold. At their touch, we experience greatly blissful awareness of voidness. Our teacher, Kalachakra, reciting a verse and a mantra, confers a concluding water empowerment by dabbing and sprinkling water from the conch shell and giving us a sip to drink, as before. Our aggregate of deep awareness and our consciousness element are now fully empowered as Vajrasattva and Prajnaparamita.

7. Light radiates from the Vajrasattva and Prajnaparamita in our body and brings back from the mandala replicas of their counterparts there. They, as well as the other empowering figures,

dissolve into the Vajrasattva and Prajnaparamita in our body. Our teacher, Kalachakra, makes an offering to us.

8. From *BHRUM* comes a wheel, which our teacher, Kalachakra, places on the seat before us. From *A* comes a Kalachakra text, which he lays in our lap. From *AH* comes a conch shell, which he gives us to hold in our right hand. From *AH* comes a bell, which we he gives us to hold and ring in our left hand. We repeat after him several verses reaffirming our commitment to wisdom and method, ringing the bell after each verse. We prostrate and agree to do what he says.

9. The Four Appended Procedures

   a. Giving the Mantras. Our teacher, Kalachakra, informs the Buddhas that he shall bestow their mantras, and we repeat a request for them. Instantaneously we arise in the form of a full blue Kalachakra, with four faces, twenty-four arms and two legs, standing and embracing a yellow Vishvamata, with four faces, eight arms and two legs. We repeat each mantra three times. With the first repetition, a replica of the mantra at the heart of our teacher, Kalachakra, emerges from it, goes out his mouth, enters our mouth and settles around a black syllable *HUM* at our heart. With the second repetition, the mantra becomes non-differentiable from the mantra at our heart, and with the third, it is stabilized. The mantras are (1) the heart mantra: *OM AH HUM HOH HAMKSHAH MALA-WARAYA HUM PHAT* (in Tibetan "hamkshah" is pronounced "hankya" and "phat" is pronounced "pay"), (2) the near heart mantra: *OM HRANG HRING HRIRING HRUNG HRILING HRAH SVAHA* (in Tibetan "svaha" is pronounced "soha") and (3) the root mantra: *OM SHRI KALACHAKRA HUM HUM PHAT.*

   b. Giving Eye Medicine. We visualize on each of the two main eyes on our front, blue face, a black *PRAM*. Our teacher, Kalachakra, smears a tiny dab of butter on our eyes with a golden eye-spoon. We imagine that, like having a cataract removed, the dimness of our lack of awareness of voidness is removed and we gain eyes of deep awareness for achieving a conceptual understanding of voidness.

   c. Giving a Mirror. From an *AH* arises a mirror. Our teacher, Kalachakra, shows this to us, reciting verses that everything, including the Kalachakra at our hearts — referring to our clear light mind — is like an illusion, like a reflection in a mirror. This enables us to gain subsequent realization of everything to be like an illusion.

d. Giving a Set of Bow and Arrows. From *HOH* arises a set of bow and arrows, to pierce through all interference from any of the four directions or above or below, in order for us to gain non-conceptual straightforward perception of voidness during total absorption.

10. Vajra Master Empowerment

a. Our teacher, Kalachakra, clears away interference and purifies into voidness ourselves and a vajra and bell. Within a state of voidness, ourselves and the vajra are generated as a blue Vajrasattva and the bell as a blue Prajnaparamita, each sitting cross-legged without any partner, and having three faces and six arms. On the forehead of each is a white *OM*, on the throat a red *AH*, at the heart a black *HUM* and at the navel a yellow *HOH*.

b. Light radiates from the heart of our teacher, Kalachakra, and returns with deep awareness beings who merge with the two Vajrasattvas of ourselves and the vajra, and with the Prajnaparamita of the bell. The five female Buddhas in the mandala empower the Vajrasattva of the vajra and the Prajnaparamita of the bell, and each receives as a crowning ornament the seal of the principal male figure of his or her Buddha-family. Our teacher, Kalachakra, makes offerings to the Vajrasattva and Prajnaparamita of the vajra and bell. They melt into drops of bodhichitta and transform back into the vajra and bell.

c. Our teacher, Kalachakra, gives us the vajra to hold in our right hand, representing the non-discordant deep awareness of the mind of the Buddhas, inseparable from voidness as its object. This confers the close bond for our mind. He gives us the bell to hold in our left hand, representing the proclamation of voidness. We ring the bell and recite a verse about voidness. This confers the close bond for our speech. Then we think how our body, as a Vajrasattva, is the appearance to which blissful deep awareness of voidness naturally gives rise. This is the great seal (*mahamudra*) of a Buddha-figure's body and is the close bond for our body. We cross our arms, holding vajra and bell, while thinking this and experiencing greatly blissful awareness of voidness.

d. Our teacher, Kalachakra, reciting a verse and a mantra, confers a concluding water empowerment by dabbing and sprinkling water from the conch shell and giving us a sip to drink, as before. We receive as a crowning ornament the seal of Akshobhya, the principal male figure of our Buddha-family. Our teacher, Kalachakra, makes offerings to us.

11. Showing the Pure Measures of the Dharma

a. Showing the Interpretable and Definitive Meanings of the Pure Measures of the Close Bonds. Our teacher, Kalachakra, explains the interpretable and definitive levels of the closely bonding practices, specific to Kalachakra, for the six Buddha-family traits.

b. Our teacher, Kalachakra, explains that the subsequent permission empowerment, received facing his yellow deep awareness face, is analogous to teaching a child to read. It purifies the stains of the deep awareness drop and, together with its appended sections, grants the ability to achieve positive potential equivalent to someone with a seventh bodhisattva level of mind.

c. He further explains that all seven empowerments given from a powdered sand mandala are called water empowerments since a cleansing action with water to purify negative potentials follows each. The seven all together empower us to meditate on the generation stage path and to achieve the final actual attainments of Akanishta, the State Beneath Nothing Else. We become laypersons (*upasaka*) of the tantra. If we keep all the vows purely for seven lifetimes, we at minimum become a lord of the seventh bodhisattva level of mind. We cross our arms and repeat a mantra, feeling the pride of all this being so.

d. Understanding the Time of Receiving the Empowerment. Our teacher, Kalachakra, explains the time of the empowerment, with all the astrological references.

e. Final Advice to Stop Any Root Downfalls. Our teacher, Kalachakra, explains that if we commit a downfall and lose our tantric vows, and if we have only received these seven empowerments, we repeat 36,000 times the mantra of the Buddha-figure on which our flower fell. To restore our vows, we re-enter the mandala — either during a Kalachakra initiation or, if we have completed the Kalachakra retreat of hundreds of thousands of mantras, with self-initiation — and take once more the seven empowerments of entering like a child. Our teacher, Kalachakra, explains the fourteen root tantric vows according to Kalachakra. We repeat three times that we shall practice exactly as he says, recite a verse of rejoicing and offer a mandala in thanksgiving.

Bibliography

MAJOR TIBETAN AND SANSKRIT SOURCES CONSULTED

Ashvaghosha II (Aśvaghoṣa; rTa-dbyangs). *Gurupañcāśatikā* (Bla-ma lnga-bcu-pa; Fifty Stanzas on the Spiritual Teacher).

Butön (Bu-ston Rin-chen grub). *dBang-gi le'u'i 'grel-bshad dri-ma med-pa'i 'od mchan-bcas* (An Explanation of the "Empowerment" Chapter of *Stainless Light*, Together with a Line-by-Line Correlation [with the Root Text]).

_____. *'Jig-rten khams-kyi le'u'i 'grel-bshad dri-ma med-pa'i 'od mchan-bcas* (An Explanation of the "World Sphere" Chapter of *Stainless Light*, Together with a Line-by-Line Correlation [with the Root Text]).

_____. *Nang-gi le'u'i 'grel-bshad dri-ma med-pa'i 'od mchan-bcas* (An Explanation of the "Internal [Kalachakra]" Chapter of *Stainless Light*, Together with a Line-by-Line Correlation [with the Root Text]).

_____. *dPal dus-kyi 'khor-lo'i dkyil-chog-gi zin-bris* (Notes on the Mandala Ritual of Glorious Kalachakra).

_____. *dPal dus-kyi 'khor-lo'i dkyil-chog yon-tan kun-'byung* (The Mandala Ritual of Glorious Kalachakra: The Source of All Good Qualities).

Seventh Dalai Lama (rGyal-dbang bsKal-bzang rgya-mtsho). *bCom-ldan-'das dpal dus-kyi 'khor-lo'i sku-gsung-thugs yongs-su rdzogs-pa'i dkyil-'khor-gyi dbang-chen cho-ga* (The Ritual for the Grand Empowerment into the Complete Mandala of the Enlightening Body, Speech and Mind of Lordly, Glorious Kalachakra).

_____. *dPal gsang-ba 'dus-pa mi-bskyod rdo-rje'i dkyil-'khor-gyi cho-ga'i rnam-par bshad-pa dbang-don de-nyid yang-gsal snang-ba rdo-rje sems-dpa'i zhal-lung* (An Explanation of the Mandala Ritual of Glorious Guhyasamaja, Illumination Clarifying the Actual Meaning of Empowerment: The Oral Tradition of Vajrasattva).

Fourteenth Dalai Lama (rGyal-dbang bsTan-'dzin rgya-mtsho) and Yongdzin Ling Rinpochey (Yongs-'dzin gLing Thub-bstan lung-rtogs rnam-rgyal 'phrin-las). *Thun-drug-dang 'brel-ba'i dus-'khor bla-ma'i rnal-'byor dpag-bsam yongs-'du'i snye-ma* (Kalachakra Guru-yoga in Conjunction with Six-session Practice: A Cluster of Fruit from an All-Embracing Wish-Granting Tree).

Desi Sanggyay-gyatso (sDe-srid Sangs-rgyas rgya-mtsho). *Vaiḍūrya sngon-po* (Blue Aquamarine).

Detri (sDe-khri 'Jam-dbyangs thub-bstan nyi-ma). *dPal dus-kyi 'khor-lo'i bskyed-rim-gyi rnam-bzhag 'jam-dpal zhal-lung* (A Presentation of the Generation Stage of Glorious Kalachakra: The Oral Tradition of Manjushri).

Dharmakirti (Dharmakirti; Chos-kyi grags-pa). *Pramāṇavārttika* (Tshad-ma rnam-'grel; A Commentary on [Dignaga's "Compendium of] Validly Cognizing Minds").

Drongtsey Yongdzin ('Brong-rtse Yongs-'dzin Blo-bzang tshul-khrims). *dPal dus-kyi 'khor-lo'i rim-gnyis-kyi lam zung-mjug bgrod-pa'i them-skas-pa* (The Path of the Two Stages of Glorious Kalachakra: Steps Leading to Unity).

Gyeltsabjey (rGyal-tshab rJe Dar-ma rin-chen). *dPal dus-kyi 'khor-lo'i rim-pa gnyis ji-ltar nyams-su len-pa'i tshul bde-ba chen-po'i lam-du myur-du 'jug-pa* (The Way to Practice the Two Stages of Glorious Kalachakra: Quickly Entering the Path of Great Bliss).

Third Karmapa (Kar-ma-pa Rang-byung rdo-rje). *rNal-'byor bla-na med-pa'i rgyud-sde rgya-mtsho'i snying-po bsdus-pa zab-mo nang-gi don* (The Meaning of the Profound "Internal [Kalachakra" Chapter of *Stainless Light*] that Gathers Together the Essence of Oceans of Anuttarayoga Tantras).

Kaydrub Norzang-gyatso (mKhas-grub Nor-bzang rgya-mtsho). *Dam-tshig gsal-ba'i sgron-me* (A Lamp to Illuminate the Closely Bonding Practices).

_____. *Phyi-nang-gzhan-gsum gsal-bar byed-pa dri-med 'od-kyi rgyan* (An Adornment for the *Stainless Light*, Clarifying the External, Internal and Alternative [Kalachakras]).

Kaydrubjey (mKhas-grub rJe dGe-legs dpal-bzang-po). *dPal dus-kyi 'khor-lo'i cho-ga dgongs-pa rab-gsal* (The Mandala Ritual of Glorious Kalachakra: Clarifying the Intended Meaning).

_____. *dPal dus-kyi 'khor-lo'i 'grel-chen dri-med 'od-kyi rgya-cher bshad-pa de-kho-na-nyid snang-bar byed-pa* (An Extensive Explanation of the *Stainless Light* Grand Commentary to Glorious Kalachakra: Illuminating the Actual State).

Kongtrül ('Jam-mgon Kong-sprul Blo-gros mtha'-yas). *rNal-'byor bla-na med-pa'i rgyud-sde rgya-mtsho'i snying-po bsdus-pa zab-mo nang-gi don nyung-ngu'i tshig-gis rnam-par 'grel-ba zab-don snang-byed* (Illuminating the Profound Meaning: A Commentary in Few Words on [the Third Karmapa's] *The Meaning of the Profound "Internal [Kalachakra" Chapter of* Stainless Light] *that Gathers Together the Essence of Oceans of Anuttarayoga Tantras*).

_____. *dPal dus-kyi 'khor-lo sku-gsung-thugs yongs-rdzogs-kyi dkyil-'khor-du byis-pa 'jug-pa'i dbang-bskur bklags-chog-tu bkod-pa ye-shes rgya-mtsho'i bcud-'dren* (Conferring the Empowerments of Entering Like a Child into the Complete Body, Speech and Mind Mandala of Glorious Kalachakra, Arranged for Study: Extracting the Essence from the Ocean of Deep Awareness).

_____. *Shes-bya kun-khyab* (An Encyclopedia of All That Can Be Known).

Kyenrab-norbu (mKhyen-rab nor-bu). *Rigs-ldan snying-thig* (The Essential Drop [Teachings] of the Kalki [Rulers of Shambhala]).

Mipam ('Ju Mi-pham 'Jam-dbyangs rnam-rgyal rgya-mtsho). *dPal dus-kyi 'khor-lo'i rgyud-kyi tshig-don rab-tu gsal-byed rdo-rje nyi-ma'i snang-ba* (The Illumination of the Diamond-strong Sun Clarifying the Literal Meaning of the Glorious Kalachakra Tantra).

Naropa (Nāropa; Nā-ro-pa). *Sekoddeśaṭīkā* (dBang-dor bstan-pa'i 'grel-pa; A Commentary Explaining the "Initiation" [Chapter of the *Root Kalachakra Tantra*]).

Ngari Panchen (mNga'-ris Paṇ-chen Padma dbang-rgyal). *Rang-bzhin rdzogs-pa chen-po'i lam-gyi cha-lag sdom-gsum rnam-nges* (Ascertaining the Three Levels of Vowed Restraints that are Branches of the Natural Path of Dzogchen).

Ngülchu Darma-badra (dNgul-chu Dharmabhadra). *Thun-drug-gi rnal-'byor mdor-bsdus-pa* (An Extremely Abbreviated Six-session Yoga).

Ngülchu Jedrung Lozang-tendzin (dNgul-chu rJe-drung Blo-bzang bstan-'dzin). *Thun-drug-gi rnal-'byor bsdus-pa* (An Abbreviated Six-session Yoga).

Pabongka (Pha-bong-kha Byams-pa bstan-'dzin 'phrin-las rgya-mtsho). *Thun-drug-gi rnal-'byor rgyas-pa* (An Extensive Six-session Yoga).

First Panchen Lama (Paṇ-chen Blo-bzang chos-kyi rgyal-mtshan). *dPal dus-kyi 'khor-lo'i 'grel-chen dri-ma med-pa'i 'od-kyi rgya-cher bshad-pa de-kho-na-nyid snang-bar byed-pa'i snying-po yid-bzhin-gyi nor-bu* (Wish-granting Gem: The Essence of [Kaydrubjey's] *An Extensive Explanation of the* Stainless Light *Grand Commentary to Glorious Kalachakra: Illuminating the Actual State*).

_____. *Thun-drug rnal-sbyor* (Six-session Yoga).

Pundarika (Kulika Puṇḍarīka, Rigs-ldan Pad-ma dkar-po). *Vimālaprabhā-nāma-laghu-kālachakra-tantra-rāja-ṭīkā* (bsDus-pa'i rgyud-kyi rgyal-po dus-kyi 'khor-lo'i 'grel-bshad dri-ma med-pa'i 'od; Stainless Light: A Commentary Explaining *The Regal Abbreviated Kalachakra Tantra*).

Tagtsang Lotsawa (sTag-tshang Lo-tsa-ba Shes-rab rin-chen). *Dus-'khor spyi-don bstan-pa'i rgya-mtsho* (An Ocean of Teachings on the General Meaning of Kalachakra).

Tsongkapa (Tsong-kha-pa Blo-bzang grags-pa). *Byang-chub sems-dpa'i tshul-khrims-kyi rnam-bshad byang-chub gzhung-lam* (An Explanation of Bodhisattvas' Ethical Discipline: The Main Path to Enlightenment).

_____. *gSang-sngags-kyi rim-pa chen-mo* (A Grand Presentation of the Stages of Secret Mantra).

_____. *gSang-sngags-kyi tshul-khrims-kyi rnam-bshad dngos-grub-kyi snye-ma* (An Explanation of Secret Mantra Ethical Discipline: A Cluster of Fruit of Actual Attainments).

SELECTED LITERATURE IN WESTERN LANGUAGES

Abegg, M. Emil. *Der Messiasglaube in Indien und Iran auf Grund der Quellen dargestellt.* Berlin and Leipzig: Walter de Gruyter & Co., 1928.

Ali, Syed Muzafer. *The Geography of the Purānas.* New Delhi: People's Publishing House, 1966.

Bernbaum, Edwin. *The Mythic Journey and Its Symbolism*: A Study of the Development of Buddhist Guidebooks to Śambhala in Relation to Their Antecedents in Hindu Mythology. Unpublished Ph.D. Dissertation, University of California, Berkeley, 1985.

_____. *The Way to Shambhala.* New York: Anchor Books, 1980.

Berzin, Alexander. "Buddhista Tantra" in *Dharma-füzetek 5.* Budapest: Buddhista Föiskola, 1996, 1-46.

_____. *Guidelines for Receiving the Kalacakra Empowerment.* Seattle: Dharma Friendship Foundation, 1989.

_____. *Einführung in das Kalachakra-Tantra.* Jägerndorf, Germany: Aryatara Institut, 1985.

_____. *Einführung in Tantra.* Munich: Aryatara Institut, 1993.

_____. "Enseñanza sobre Tantra" in *Nagaryuna,* no. 30, Valencia, Spain, July-Sept. 1995, 15-22.

_____. "Introduccion a los Compromisos y su Significado" in *Nagaryuna,* no. 3, Valencia, Spain, Oct.-Nov. 1988, 24-27.

_____. *Introduction à l'Initiation de Kalatchakra.* Lavaur, France: Institut Vajrayogini, 1986.

_____. "An Introduction to Tibetan Astronomy and Astrology" in *Tibet Journal,* vol. 12, no. 1, Dharamsala, Spring 1987.

_____. "Kalachakra Initiatie" in *Maitreya Magazine,* vol. 7, no. 2, Emst, Holland, 1985.

_____. "Tibetan Astro Studies" in *Chö-Yang,* Year of Tibet Edition, Dharamsala, 1991, 181-192.

_____. "Tibetan Astrology and Astronomy" in *Maitreya Magazine,* vol. 11, no. 4, Emst, Holland, 1989.

_____. "Tibetaanse Sternenkunde en Astrologie" in *Maitreya Magazine,* vol. 7, no. 3, Emst, Holland, 1985.

_____. "Tibetische Astro-Wissenschaften: Dem Karma auf der Spur" in *Tibet und Buddhismus*, vol. 40, Hamburg Germany, January-March, 1997.

_____. "Uvod u tibetsku astronomiju i astrologiju" in *Kulture Istoka*, vol. 10, Beograd, October-December, 1986.

_____. "Visualisatie" in *Maitreya Magazine*, vol. 9, no. 2, Emst, Holland, 1987.

Brauen, Martin. *Das Mandala:* Der heilige Kreis im tantrischen Buddhismus. Koln: DuMont, 1992.

Bryant, Barry. *The Wheel of Time Sand Mandala*: Visual Scripture of Tibetan Buddhism. San Francisco: Harper Collins, 1995.

Bryant, Barry and Yignyen, Tenzin. *Process of Initiation*: The Indo-Tibetan Rite of Passage into Shambala: The Kalachakra Initiation. New York: Samaya Foundation and Namgyel Monastery, 1990.

Del Vico, Enrico (ed.). *Kalachakra*. Rome: Editalia Edizioni d'Italia, 1996.

Dhargyey, Geshe Ngawang, "Introduction à l'Initiation de Kalachakra" in *Le Tibet Journal*. Anduze, France: Editions Dharma, 1985.

_____. "Introduction to the Kalacakra Initiation" in *Tibet Journal*, vol. 1, no. 1, Dharamsala, July-September 1975; reprinted in *Kalachakra Initiation, Madison, 1981*. Madison, Wisconsin: Deer Park Books, 1985.

_____. *Kalachakra Tantra*. Dharamsala: Library of Tibetan Works and Archives, 1985.

Dikshit, K. N. "Buddhist Centres in Afghanistan" in *India's Contribution to World Thought and Culture*, ed. Lokesh Chandra, et al. Madras: Vivekananda Rock Memorial Committee, 1970, 229-238.

Dudjom Rinpoche. *Perfect Conduct: Ascertaining the Three Vows*, with root text by Ngari Panchen. Boston: Wisdom Publications, 1996.

Grönbold, Günter. "Materialien zur Geschichte des Sadanga Yoga II: Die Offenbarung des Sadanga-yoga im Kalachakra-System," in *Central Asiatic Journal*, vol. 28, nos. 1-2 (1984), 43-56.

_____. "Materialien zur Geschichte des Sadanga Yoga III: Der sechsgliederige Yoga des Kalacakra Tantras," in *Asiatische Studien*, vol. 37, no. 1 (1983), 25-45.

Grünwedel, Albert. *Der Weg nach Śambhala*. *(Abhandlung der Königlich Bayerischen Akademie der Wissenschaften*, vol. 29, no. 3). Munich: 1915.

Hodgson, Marshall G. S. *The Venture of Islam:* Conscience and History in a World Civilization, 3 vols. (vol 1: *The Classical Age of Islam*). Chicago: University of Chicago Press, 1974.

Hoffmann, Helmut. "Buddha's Preaching of the Kālacakra Tantra at the Stūpa of Dhānyakataka" in *German Scholars on India*, vol. 1. Varanasi: Chowkhambha Sanskrit Series Office, 1973, 136-140.

_____. "Das Kalacakra, die letzte Phase des Buddhismus in Indien," *Saeculum*, vol. 15 (1964), 125-131.

_____. "Kalacakra Studies I: Manichaeism, Christianity and Islam in the Kalacakra Tantra," in *Central Asiatic Journal*, vol. 13, no. 1 (1969), 52-73. "Kalacakra Studies I: Addenda et Corrigenda," *Central Asiatic Journal*, vol. 15, no. 4 (1972), 298-301.

_____. "Literaturhistorische Bemerkungen zur Sekoddeśaṭīkā des Nadapāda" in *Beiträge zur indischen Philologie und Altertumskunde*, zum 70. Geburtstag dargebracht von der deutschen Indologie, ed. Walther Schubring. Hamburg: Cram, De Gruyter, 1951, 140-147.

_____. "Manichaeism and Islam in the Buddhist Kalacakra System," in *Proceedings of the IXth International Congress of the History of Religions 1958*. Tokyo: 1960, 96-99.

Kalachakra Initiation, Madison, 1981. Madison, Wisconsin: Deer Park Books, 1985.

Kalu Rinpoche. *The Kalachakra Empowerment*: Taught by the Venerable Kalu Rinpoche. Vancouver: Kagyu Kunkhyab Choling, 1986.

Kamtrul, Garjang, "Geographie et Histoire de Shambhala" in *Le Tibet Journal*. Anduze, France: Editions Dharma, 1985.

_____. "The History and Geography of Shambhala" in *Tibet Journal*, vol. 1, no. 1, Dharamsala, July-September 1975.

Kollmar, Paulenz. "Utopian Thought in Tibetan Buddhism: A Survey of the Śambhala Concept and Its Sources," in *Studies in Central and East Asian Religions*, vol. 5/6 (1992/3), 78-96.

Kuwayama, Shoshin. "The Turki Śāhis and Relevant Brahmanical Sculptures in Afghanistan," in *East and West*, vol. 26, nos. 3-4 (September-December 1976), 375-408.

Mullin, Glenn H. *The Practice of Kalachakra*. Ithaca: Snow Lion, 1991.

Nadapada. *Iniziazione: Kalachakra/Naropa*: a cura di Raniero Gnoli e Giacomella Orofino. (*Bibioteca Orientale*, no. 1). Milan: Adelphi, 1994.

Newman, John. "Buddhist Sanskrit in the Kālacakra Tantra," in *Journal of the International Association of Buddhist Studies*, vol. 11, no. 1 (1988), 123-140.

_____. *The Outer Wheel of Time*: Vajrayāna Buddhist Cosmology in the Kālacakra Tantra. Unpublished Ph.D. Dissertation, University of Wisconsin, 1987.

_____. "The *Paramādibuddha* (the Kālacakra *Mūlatantra*) and Its Relation to the Early Kālacakra Literature," in *Indo-Iranian Journal*, vol. 30 (1987), 93-102.

Nihom, N. "Notes on the Origin of Some Quotations in the Sekoddeśatīkā of Nāḍapāda," in *Indo-Iranian Journal*, vol. 27 (1984), 17-26.

Orofino, Giacomella. *Sekoddeśa*: A Critical Edition of the Tibetan Translations. (*Serie Orientale Roma*, no. 72). Roma: Istituto Italiano per il Medio ed Estremo Oriente, 1994.

Polichetti, Massimiliano A. "Il Sitema di Kalachakra e le caratteristiche del Buddismo Tibetano" in *L'immagine Tibetana del Tempo*, Il Mandala di Sabbie Colorate di Kalachakra (ed. Eugenio La Rocca). (*Comune di Roma Ripartizione*, no. 10). Rome: Acquario Romano, 1993, 19-28.

Reigle, David. *Kalacakra Sadhana and Social Responsibility*. Santa Fe: Spirit of the Sun Publications, 1996.

_____. *The Lost Kālacakra Mūla Tantra on the Kings of Śambhala*. (*Kālacakra Research Publications*, no. 1). Talent, Oregon: Eastern School, 1986.

Rivière, Jean N. *Kalachakra: initiation tantrique du Dalaï Lama*. Paris: Éditions Robert Laffont, 1985.

Roerich, Nicholas. *Shambhala: The Heart of Asia*. New York: Roerich Museum Press, 1930.

Schuh, Dieter. *Untersuchungen zur Geschichte der tibetischen Kalenderrechnung*. (*Verzeichnis der Orientalischen Handschriften in Deutschlands*. Supplementband 16). Wiesbaden: Franz Steiner Verlag, 1973.

Scott, David Alan. "The Iranian Face of Buddhism," in *East and West*, vol. 41, nos. 1-4 (December 1991), 43-78.

Sopa, Geshe Lhundub; Jackson, Roger; and Newman, John. *The Wheel of Time, The Kalachakra in Context*. Madison, Wisconsin: Deer Park Books, 1985.

Sparham, Gareth. *An Explanation of Ethical Standards in Secret Mantra Called "Fruit Cluster of Accomplishments."* Unpublished manuscript.

Tatz, Mark, trans. *Asanga's Chapter of Morality with the Commentary of Tsong-khapa*. Lewiston: Mellen Press, 1986.

Tenzin Gyatso, the Dalai Lama and Hopkins, Jeffrey. *The Kalachakra Tantra: Rite of Initiation for the Stage of Generation*. London: Wisdom Publications, 1985.

Wilson, Horace Hayman, trans. *The Vishnu Purana: A System of Hindu Mythology and Tradition*. London: Trübner & Co., 1864; reprinted, New York: Garland Publishing, 1981.

Kalachakra and Other Six-session Yoga Texts

A small booklet entitled *Kalachakra and Other Six-session Yoga Texts* by Alexander Berzin is available from Snow Lion Publications. It contains translations of the following texts:

1) *An Extremely Abbreviated Six-session Yoga* by Ngulchu Darma-badra
2) *An Abbreviated Six-session Yoga* by Ngulchu Jedrung Lozang-tendzin
3) *An Extensive Six-session Yoga* by the First Panchen Lama
4) *Kalachakra Guru-yoga in Conjunction with Six-session Practice* by the Fourteenth Dalai Lama and versified by Yongdzin Ling Rinpochey

Snow Lion Publications
P.O. Box 6483
Ithaca, NY 14851
Tel: 800-950-0313 Orders only, or 607-273-8519
Fax: 607-273-8508
http://www.snowlionpub.com